I Remember Sunnyside

The Rise & Fall of a Magical Era

Revised Edition

by Mike Filey

The Dundurn Group
Toronto and Oxford
1996

We would like to express our gratitude to the **Canada Council,** the **Ontario Arts Council,** and the **Book Publishing Industry Development Program** of the **Department of Communication** for their generous assistance and ongoing support.

Care has been taken to trace the ownership of copyright material used in the text (including the illustrations). The author and publisher welcome any information enabling them to rectify any reference or credit in subsequent editions.

J. Kirk Howard, Publisher

Canadian Cataloguing in Publication Data

Filey, Mike, 1941 –
       I remember Sunnyside

Revised Edition
Includes bibliographical references.
ISBN 1-55002-274-1

1. Sunnyside Amusement Park (Toronto, Ont.) -
History. I. Title.
GV433.C33T67   790' .06'8713541   C96-932162-7

Cover illustration: Herb Franklin
Editor: Nadine Stoikoff
Designer: Ron & Ron Design and Photography
Printer: Webcom

Second Printing, April 1998

Dundurn Press	Dundurn Press	Dundurn Press
8 Market Street, Suite 200	73 Lime Walk	250 Sonwil Drive
Toronto, Ontario	Headington, Oxford	Buffalo, New York
M5E 1M6	England 0X3 7AD	U.S.A. 14225

Dedication

To my grandmother, Martha Hatch, who first took me to "the playground by the lake," and to my mother and father who kept taking me back.

    This revised edition is also dedicated to the memory of those who assisted with the original work and have since passed away.

Contents

A train of ecstatic passengers on the Sunnyside Flyer roller-coaster roars by overhead as traffic pauses at the Lakeshore pedestrian crossover. The young fellow with the briefcase was on his way to earn a few dollars painting the owners' initials in gold paint on the doors of their flivvers. The former Sunnyside Orphanage, recently converted into the new St. Joseph's Hospital (and now St. Joseph's Health Centre) can be seen on the hill in the background to the left.

This same view, as depicted by talented Burlington, Ontario, artist Herb Franklin, appears on the cover. Herb, who spent his early years in the Ossington/Dupont part of Toronto, records his memories of Sunnyside in his self-published book *Street Stories of Toronto*. Information on purchasing the book can be obtained by writing Herb, c/o 626 Fothergill Boulevard, Burlington, Ontario L7L 6E3.

Foreword
Robert Thomas Allen

One bright, still, hazy day I walked down past some beautiful willows at Sunnyside to a peaceful spot on the shore behind the bathing pavilion and sat at a battered old picnic table eating a hot dog and watching three kids skipping stones. In the distance I could hear the moan, hiss, growl, and whine of fourteen lanes of fast traffic. The fresh smell of the lake and of warm paint made me drowsy and I began to doze and my thought drifted back to the days of the old amusement park that used to be here and I imagined what I heard wasn't traffic, but the rumble and roar of the rides – the whip, the Derby racer, the roller-coaster – and the ecstatic screams of the girls (they must be all around seventy now).

You'd take a streetcar and get off at the station restaurant, where the *Lakeshore* streetcars headed southwest across a bridge over the railway tracks, and you'd go down a long set of stairs into the smell of gun smoke, perfume, french fries, popcorn, and sparks from the Dodgem, and submerge into a crowd of fellow humans, as relaxing as sinking into a warm tub, and shuffle along past the weight-guesser, the rabbit run, the poker game, and fish pond – the hoarse cries of front men exclaiming over the amazing skill of their customers and how close they were coming to winning prizes. The merry-go-round was a shadowy, breezy cave of polished brass and mirrors and carved wood where you could ride around on a charger, or a camel, holding onto a brass pole or sit in the Roman chariot one arm over the back like a debauched emperor, lulled by music and the faint breeze, with your worries flung gently outward by centrifugal force, sometimes falling in love with some girl who was waiting her turn, who floated past you rhythmically like someone in a lovely séance. There were two merry-go-rounds at Sunnyside: the Derby racer, now at the Canadian National Exhibition, and the Menagerie merry-go-round, which is now in Disneyland, California. Another magnificent Toronto merry-go-round that used to be at Toronto Island is now in Walt Disney World in Florida.

We didn't know it then, but we were in something more than a crowd at Sunnyside; we were in the mainstream of major sociological change. Sunnyside came in with the automobile – not with the early models of the 1890s, but with the beginning of the automotive age when cars were to change our cities and our lives. The automobile was a magic carpet that smelled of rubber curtains and gasoline, the new smell of the future, progress, and adventure, and it invoked thoughts of remote country roads and shimmering lakes and far-off wonderful places of an exciting world.

We were still very aware of the marvel of being able to, say, drive down the Danforth or Bloor Street for a brick of ice cream and be back in some fabulous time, like eight minutes; and of the miraculous fact that you could get into your Ford coupé outside your house, and sit comfortably behind a steering wheel until you reached Sunnyside, stop at the curb, pull on the emergency brake, and step out fifteen, twenty feet from, say, the shooting gallery. But Sunnyside created some of the first great traffic jams. There was one cop, with a hand-operated wooden stop-and-go sign shaped something like a living-room floor lamp. It was the first time somebody told you when you could move, and you got the feeling as you sat there looking at the line of cars, moving bumper to bumper about three feet at a time, with people eating ice cream cones stepping between the bumpers, that the whole world had gone mad. Men used to teach their wives to drive in those days and they would make them drive through Sunnyside on a busy warm evening, figuring that by the time they got from the Humber River to the Palais Royale they'd never forget how to change gears again, and I know women approaching their gold wedding anniversary who have never forgiven their husbands for this, and probably never will.

Sunnyside went through the Great Depression and into the beginning of the age of affluence. Over half that time, money was regarded as a precise gauge of value and a commodity hard to come by. It had absolute value. If someone had said when you spent, for instance, thirty cents on a ring-toss game without winning anything, that it was only a little bit of money, it would have been like saying it was only a little bit of your arm. You were prepared to lose it, but not to think of it as nothing. Your pay came folded in a flat brown envelope the size of a playing card, which during the Depression sometimes had a white slip in it saying that you were fired. You *saved* for an afternoon or evening at Sunnyside or any other place, sometimes dropping nickels and dimes in banks designed like little stoves and steam engines and made of solid iron to encourage thrift, and when you got fed up with frugality you had to get the bank down on the cellar floor with a cold chisel and a hammer to get your money out.

The age of affluence started about ten years before the end of Sunnyside when people out for dinner began leaving little untidy piles of bills in the middle of the table for tips, and prices began to be raised without apology or explanation, and kids began carrying around more money than I had after I'd reached adulthood. "I've got thirteen dollars in my wallet," I heard one youngster headed for Sunnyside pool tell a friend a while ago, as if making a flat statement of poverty, mentioning an amount two dollars more than I was making a week when I got married. I'll say one thing, though, about another kid who was ahead of me in a line-up the same day to buy an ice cream cone for forty cents; he tried to talk the girl into giving it to him for a quarter. He didn't, but I got the feeling listening to him that money was coming back in style.

We paraded along the Sunnyside boardwalk at Easter in new suits, shoes, socks, garters, hats, shirts, ties, topcoats, and braces with no idea that attitudes to clothes were on the verge of drastic changes, and that during the existence of Sunnyside the ideal look would shift from something suggesting old money and landed gentry, to the styles that began when, following the example of Bing Crosby, men began leaving their shirts out because it was more comfortable, and ended with the frayed, patched, faded appearance suggesting open roads and jailhouses and guitars. You would never see a man or woman at Sunnyside without a hat. Blue jeans hadn't arrived (except as work clothes for cowboys). Clothes were kept neat and pressed and shoes shined. If you took your girl out in a canoe from Dean's Sunnyside Pleasure Boats you took off your jacket and folded it on a thwart and perhaps loosened your tie, but left your hat on. A young fellow took great pride in the way his hat was tinted, running his thumb and third finger along the crown to make geometrically parallel troughs. If a man put off getting a haircut until his hair reached his ears, he was considered to be someone lacking in moral fibre, like someone who had kept putting off fixing a back porch until it collapsed. Bathing suits were demure, with legs that came halfway down the thighs and had little skirts for the sake of modesty. It was against the law for men to go bare chested, and if any girl had appeared at the bathing pavilion on one of today's bikinis, a cop would have walked over to her with long strides, thrown his tunic around her, and taken her down to the station. But it's a mistake to think that people looked funny in those days. They do in photographs, due partly to the state of photography and partly to some mysterious psychological process I don't understand, but they didn't then. Bathing beauties looked beautiful and maddening and slightly sinful, and so did the girls in the Charleston contests.

Sunnyside Amusement Park fitted as if in the crook of an arm along a curve of the lake from about a mile west of the Canadian National Exhibition to the Humber. Its predecessor was Scarboro Beach Park in east Toronto where I remember coasting down a polished, inclined wooden floor known as "the bumps" and riding lean, flat-nosed boats down a chute and aquaplaning onto a pond in a wild, rock-ing, bucking explosion of water, and going on a roller coaster with the genteel name of "the scenic railway." The amusement park of our parents' day was Hanlan's Point. Sunnyside was a raggedy weedy shore with rows of beautiful slender green Lombardy poplars and clay cliffs thirty feet high, of great interest to students of Toronto's world-famous glacial deposits. In the days when women carried parasols and wore ankle-length dresses and hats as big as bicycle wheels decorated with things like artificial grapes, there was a wooden sidewalk and some ramshackle bathing houses and a canoe club up on pilings over the water. A dirt road ran along beside the Canadian National and Grand Trunk Railway. In 1917 the Toronto Harbour Commission began filling the shore with sand pumped from the lake bottom, and the land was graded by horse-drawn steel scoops that the labourer gripped by two handles like a plow. The horse still did much of the world's work when Sunnyside began. Construction started on the Menagerie merry-go-round in 1921 and it was ready in 1922, along with a splendid new bathing pavilion.

In 1922, Sunnyside was officially opened by Mayor Maguire. The beach was named Sunnyside after a villa built at the south end of High Park by John Howard, who was Toronto's first surveyor, and for twenty years an art teacher at Upper Canada College. Howard's own house, an architectural valentine with three chimneys, still stands in High Park open to visitors. Much of High Park – 165 acres – was given to the city by this man 100 years ago. A promotional magazine of the early days said "Sunnyside Beach heralds the greatness of this Canadian metropolis." It opened each year on May 24, Queen Victoria's birthday, when the lake was so cold that when you waded in you felt as if somebody had grabbed you underwater, which was the reason for the eventual construction of Sunnyside pool, in which the water temperatures could be controlled.

Sunnyside was closed on Sundays, and shut down tight at twelve midnight Saturday night. No alcoholic drinks were ever sold there. This wasn't so surprising; there were no drinking places anywhere in Toronto until 1934, when the government began licensing hotels to serve beer and wine. By the time bars and liquor lounges came to Toronto, Sunnyside was closed. What was surprising was that Sunnyside had no ice cream parlours, at least in the amusement park; there was one in Sunnyside Pavilion, a fancy dine and dance place which became successively the Club Esquire and Club Top Hat. It had been there since 1917, at first on the shore but, as the land was filled in, further and further inland. Ice cream parlours were where the action was those days – often rich old mahogany and marble grottos with Tiffany lamps, where you could get dishes with names like Love in Bloom, A Night in June, Merry Widow, Tin Roof, Tutti Frutti, and Moon Over Miami. One woman who worked at Sunnyside, and to whom I talked over the phone, gave me her theory as to why there were no ice cream parlours at Sunnyside. "They were too sophisticated for us," she said with a fond whoop of amusement.

Sunnyside went in for a few awful ideas, like flag-pole sitting, contests for dogs dressed up in doll clothes, diving horses, bears on bicycles, and burning Island ferry-boats and Great Lakes sailing ships, like *Lyman M. Davis*, as a public attraction. But for the most part it did nobody any harm and probably did a lot of good; let people go around in circles to music, try to acquire some fabulous treasure without working for it, drink Vernor's Ginger Ale and Honey Dew and Pineapple Kiss and become for a moment taller, faster, and fancier on roller skates. But the space was needed for the automobile. Politicians thought it was a disgraceful obstacle to progress and made speeches about it. Sunnyside wound down, gave a last wheeze and toot on the calliope of the merry-go-round, and came to a stop, and in late 1955 workmen began tearing it down.

A while ago I looked in through the locked front door of the Palais Royale, a white clapboard building with a blue roof at the east end of the park. A man doing something around some boats had told me that dances were still held there. A door on the opposite side of the big dance floor was open so that I could see the tables silhouetted against the bright light of the lake, and a soft reflection from the polished dance floor, and I rang the bell and nobody answered, and I was kind of glad they didn't, for I was already inside in my imagination, going up the red carpeted stairs hearing for the first time, in a kind of trance, at firsthand some legendary band that until then we'd heard only on records or radio – like Tommy Dorsey's or Bob Crosby's – making some of the most exciting sounds ever devised by man and I left, a fresh breeze from the lake lifting the corners of a few bits of paper, as I thought of the days of Sunnyside when all things seemed possible and the late afternoon sun lit up the summits of the roller-coaster and you felt you were somehow at the source of things, a warm and tattered tent of life, convinced that something indescribably wonderful was going to happen within the next few minutes – the very spirit of Sunnyside.

Robert Thomas Allen was born in Toronto in 1911 and began his career in the fields of advertising and public relations. He enjoyed writing as a pastime and eventually turned his hobby into a full-time profession. Robert Thomas was the author of fourteen books and wrote countless articles that appeared in almost every major Canadian periodical. He was twice awarded the coveted Leacock Medal for Humour (The Grass is Never Greener *and* Children, Wives and Wildlife), *and in 1952 won the Governor-General's Award for his short story* "The Man We Celebrate." *Mr. Allen died on July 11, 1990. Having read his* When Toronto Was for Kids *several times, I was eager to have Robert Thomas write the preface to my book. I cherish his contribution greatly.*

Preface to Revised Edition

When this book first appeared in the fall of 1982 it was eagerly received not only by people who had actually visited Sunnyside and wanted to relive those special times, but by people who had only heard about this magical place and could only experience Sunnyside through words and photographs. In fact, the closest I ever came to having a book on the national bestseller list was as a result of the remarkably high sales figures achieved by *I Remember Sunnyside*. Over the fifteen years that have gone by since the book first appeared in stores, I have written many other books on Toronto's rich and fascinating history. Nevertheless, *I Remember Sunnyside*, now long out of print, continues to be the one book for which I receive the most requests. Now, thanks to Kirk Howard and the nice people at Dundurn Press, a revised and updated edition of *I Remember Sunnyside* is available to once again evoke nostalgic memories of being there for Sunnyside "old-timers" or, for the Sunnyside rookie, the wish that they had been there.

At Hanlan's Point **(above),** photographer William James caught King (or is it Queen?) plummeting into the clear waters of a Toronto Island lagoon in the summer of 1911.

This pair of diving horses, rather majestically named King and Queen, perhaps in honour of the recently crowned British monarchs King George V and Queen Mary, was just one example of the numerous attractions presented each summer to lure the public to the Island amusement park. An advertisement for the park in the June 17, 1911 edition of the *Star Weekly* informs the reader that "the pure white equines are descendants of the wild horses of Florida that, in times gone by, disported themselves in the everglades." The ad goes on, "The platform from which the two white horses plummet is 40 feet above the surface of the lagoon. The dive is made with lowered head and feet outstretched and is exceedingly

graceful. All this is done without a whip and with the horses own volition."

Visible in the left background is the popular scenic railway. The runways of the Toronto City Centre (formerly Toronto Island) Airport now straddle this location.

One

Early Toronto Amusement Parks

Amusement parks have been around for centuries. In the mid-1600s, what were known as "pleasure gardens" made their appearance in France, and soon, thereafter, in other cities on the European continent. The "pleasure gardens" were really nothing more than grassy clearings where beds of flowers, tree-lined pathways, the occasional fountain, and other visual embellishments were laid out to entice "pleasure seekers" to come eat, drink, and be merry. Many such gardens added various participation sports, such as lawn bowling, shuffleboard, and tennis. As the years went by some gardens introduced circus acts to further entice and entertain their customers. It wasn't uncommon to see a juggling act or two, tightrope walkers, and, of course, the daring young man on the flying trapeze. Even the world-famous International Air Show at the Canadian National Exhibition in Toronto had its forerunner as part of a pleasure garden's itinerary. Visitors to these pleasure gardens 300 years ago marvelled at the hot-air balloon ascensions and parachute jumping attractions that lacked only the noise and speed of our modern air shows, but, in their time, were every bit as exciting and nerve-wracking. Some gardens introduced music and dancing, and some even succumbed to the "evils" of gambling and liquor.

In England, the pleasure garden really started with the "evils" of liquor. Many of these early entertainment complexes grew up around pubs and taverns. One of the best known was Vauxhall Gardens in London, which opened in 1661, and quickly became an international tourist attraction, offering all the features of the continental style of pleasure garden, including music, sports, air shows, and fireworks. For almost two centuries, Vauxhall was the epitome of pleasure gardens. It closed forever with a mighty fireworks festival on July 25, 1850. While Vauxhall was headed downhill, over in Vienna, the Prater was gaining in popularity. The Prater was originally a game preserve created by Emperor Maximillian II, and in 1766 was turned over to the citizens of Vienna by Emperor Joseph II. In 1873, a World's Fair was held at the Prater and for the first time a collection of primitive (by our standards) but, nevertheless, incredibly exciting rides or "amusement Machines" were introduced to the patrons of a century ago in an area called the Wursetelprater. These rides included a German carousel, a wooden wheel (the forerunner of George Ferris' Ferris Wheel that came along several years later at the Chicago's World Fair of 1893), and the extremely popular Russian Mountain ride which consisted of small two-passenger cars rolling down an inclined track from a high point to a low point, much like

a century-old version of a simple roller-coaster. In addition to amusement machines, the Prater featured a fun house, several games of chance, many food establishments, drinking outlets, and much more that transformed the typical pleasure garden into the noisy, rollicking amusement park that had, amongst its membership, our very own Sunnyside.

Long before Sunnyside Amusement Park emerged on the scene in Toronto, several smaller, but no less exciting, amusement parks fascinated the local clientele. In 1843, the Privat Brothers, Peter and Joseph, opened on Toronto Island an early version of a Walt Disney World complex that included a hotel (without the Disney monorail) and tiny amusement park. This park was the first of its kind not only in Toronto, then called York, but in the entire province we now call Ontario. When I say it was a tiny amusement park, it was just that: a wooden carousel-type ride, a swing, a ten-pin bowling alley (five-pin was to be devised by Torontonian Tommy Ryan many years later), and a small zoo. This recreational facility was reached by a five-horsepower ferryboat (powered by five real horses), and only existed for a few years.

The next park, and the first of any major size in the city, was also on Toronto Island, this time at the westerly end, the portion known as Hanlan's Point. This park was developed by several entrepreneurs, including world champion sculler Ned Hanlan, and a fascinating fellow named Lawrence Solman, who, in addition to his Toronto Island interests, was also involved with major league baseball, the Royal Alexandra Theatre, Mutual Street Arena, and, eventually, with Sunnyside Amusement Park. Hanlan's Point was a well-equipped park with a large carousel, scenic railway, a gentle version of a roller-coaster, swing-around rides, shooting galleries and other games of skill, a tea garden and dance pavilion, and a succession of grandstands where baseball and lacrosse were played and in later years where many company and church picnics were held. Hanlan's Point flourished from the 1880s until the economic climate soured in the late twenties, culminating in the park's closure a few years later. Often given as reasons for the death of Hanlan's Point were the removal of the Maple Leaf Baseball Team to the new stadium at the foot of Bathurst Street in 1926, the development of the Island Airport, the advent of the automobile that permitted family trips further afield than ever before, and, of course, the 1922 opening of Sunnyside Amusement Park on the mainland.

During the Hanlan's Point era another park entered the picture. Situated in the Beaches area of eastern

Toronto, Scarboro Beach Park opened in 1907 as a small amusement park to serve the eastenders and to continue the traditions of its predecessors, Munro and Victoria Park. Five years later, the park was purchased by the Toronto Railway Company which expanded the facilities and ran it as a profitable trolley-park at the end of a streetcar line which promoted not only increased passenger traffic, but extended usage of their streetcar fleet in the evenings and on weekends.

A short eighteen years later Scarboro Beach, too, was bulldozed into oblivion.

When sections of the old Dundas Highway became almost impassable during the spring and fall, Lake Shore Road became a popular route to the head of the lake. As a result, several hotels were constructed at the mouth of the Humber River to serve the needs of the travelling public. Soon these hotels became popular summer resorts served by the steamers *Annie Craig* and *Waterdown*, which ran from the city to a long wooden pier just west of the Humber River. Hotels such as Devins', McDowell's,

Octavius L. Hick's Royal Oak, and John Duck's Wimbleton House **(the latter shown in this sketch)** provided not only dining and lodging facilities but entertainment in the form of dancehalls, bicycle tracks, fishponds, and small menageries. John Duck took over the roadhouse pictured above from one John Strathy in 1873 and ran it until he died in 1891. For the next two years, Duck's widow operated the hotel, which by then had new amusements such as swings and a simple merry-go-round. In 1901, Catherine Crow acquired the operation. She ran it until fire destroyed the hotel in 1912, and hence the area became known as Crow's Beach in the early years of this century. Unfortunately, it became a "Gentiles Only" bathing beach several years later. Today the Palace Pier condominium complex and several taverns and motels are situated on the site of Toronto's early amusement strip.

Victoria Park **(above),** located on a fourteen-acre wooded lot just south of Queen Street, near the present R.C. Harris water filtration plant (and at the foot of a modern thoroughfare, appropriately named Victoria Park Avenue), was another popular amusement park at the turn of the century.

It was developed in the early 1880s and financed by several prominent citizens of the day, including Alderman John Irwin, Bob Davies, and P.G. Close, and was managed by J.H. Boyle, who in later days became a prominent real estate agent in the city. The area taken over by the entrepreneurs was about six miles east of the young city and was already a popular picnic area for eastenders, who called the place "yellowbanks" because of the colour of the sandy bluffs nearby.

Each summer thousands of fun-seekers from the city would be brought directly to the little wharf at the park on the steamers *Chicoutimi* and *Steinhoff* from berths at the foot of Yonge Street. Once at the park, visitors ate their sandwiches in one of the many picnic shelters, drank their favourite beverages in the restaurant, danced in the rustic wooden pavilion, or climbed to the top of the lookout tower to survey the rural setting of the park.

Appropriately, Victoria Park always opened on Victoria Day, and visitors would stream to the park by boat, carriage, and even horse-drawn streetcar once the tracks of the old Kingston Road Tramway Company were extended down Blantyre Avenue.

Attractions at Victoria Park were numerous. Foot races were popular, with such well-known professional runners as Duke McGarry, Arthur Sparks, and Tom Chambers pitted against local citizens. These competitions created great excitement and resulted in much exchanging of money as wagers were won and lost. Another feature was tight-rope-walking exhibitions, and it was an exciting day when Harry Leslie, who had crossed the Niagara River on a tightrope, visited the park to show his skills.

Less exhausting events included donkey riding and several games of chance, the latter supervised by the local county constables Bob Melbourne and Robert Burns. They had their hands full one day when the well-known fighter Paddy Ry was set on by a gang of local toughs. During the brawl, several of the instigators were tossed bodily over the bluffs by strongman Paddy.

Other parks sprang up in competition with Victoria Park; Long Branch and Lorne Park being two. These latter parks were not as well patronized as Victoria Park and became, instead, popular summer resorts. Victoria Park passed out of existence before the turn of the century only to be resurrected a little farther to the west some ten or so years later, when Scarboro Beach Park opened in 1907.

A Toronto (not to mention a Canadian) tradition for more than a century, the Canadian National Exhibition began in 1879 as the Toronto Industrial Exhibition. From the very start, in addition to the display buildings, military band concerts, and horse shows, there have been various amusement devices to entertain the stout-of-heart. In those early days of the fair, the hand-cranked wheel (it wasn't called a Ferris Wheel until George Washington Gale Ferris patented his version in the early 1890s) was a crowd pleaser. In 1894, one year after the World's Fair with its "Midway Plaisance" was held in Chicago, the Ex introduced a multitude of amusement devices, including "Ferris wheels **(photo right)**, carousals [*sic*], swings, and other amusements for young and old." However, the Exhibition directors announced they would not tolerate "gamblers, fakers, or other objectionable persons on the grounds." Five years later the Exhibition catalogue boasted that an area known as "the Olio-de-Plaisance" (the term "midway" wouldn't do – too common!) would be locat-

ed just east of the grandstand and would be superior to any mere midway, as it was under the direct supervision of the Exhibition management. It wasn't until 1902 that the term "midway" was adopted and the rides and games finally had a home and a name that remains to the present day. In that year there was a camel ride and, over near the Stanley Barracks, the Roller Boller Chutes **(photo above)**, an attraction that was to be found in almost every major amusement park in the world.

Hanlan's Point Amusement Park.

The following article appeared in the *Globe*, Toronto, July 5th, 1888:

The Island Suburb

"For those who do not live on Toronto Island there is amusement enough to spare just now. The merry-go-round with its score or more of wooden horses and the diminutive elephants, and its wheezy out-of-tune-and-out-of-time organ, does a big business. Nor are the juveniles the only ones that patronize it. Not a bit of it. Mary Ann out for a half-holiday, the young city swell whom you would have though 'decidedly above that sort of thing,' the young mother with her first baby, and the old man himself, pay the fee and have five minutes worth of dizziness. An then there is the 'great and only museum of living curiosities,' presided over by a gentleman with strong lungs, a loud voice and slight reverence for the much-abused letter 'H.' The fat lady from Central Africa, weighing 510 pounds without her hair-pins, is on exhibition, and is alone worth the price of admission. How she reminds you of Sidney Smith's remark, when overcome by the heat, about taking off his flesh and sitting in his bones. And there is a wild girl from somewhere in South America, and a real live Zulu with an Irish accent, and no end of other curiosities. If not satiated after seeing these live wonders, there is the Switchback railway, the shooting galleries, the swings, the machines for testing your strength, and those for testing your nerves by electricity, and no end of other novelties. In the grandstand of an evening an excellent band plays and about once a week a little theatre is open for comic opera, drama, burlesque, and what not. The Island is a village in itself, with stores, churches, hotels, streets, and well planked sidewalks, wharves, and an excellent ferryboat service. What a change in less than ten years, and when all the contemplated improvements are completed how great the change again! The City has wisely secured several acres for a park, and it is being rapidly beautified and laid out. Several hundred trees were planted last year and the year before, and they are growing well. Flower beds and lawns have been laid down, terra cotta vases and other pieces of sculpture are dotted here and there, the stagnant lagoon is being filled up, and the Island Park will soon be second to none of the smaller parks around the City. Taking it all in all, Toronto Island is as pleasant a place for a picnic, a day's rest, or for a summer residence as can be found anywhere in Canada, and no wonder other cities regret they have not such a spot!"

In 1880 Edward Hanlan, who had just become the world's greatest sculler by defeating Edward Trickett on the Thames River in England, built a large hotel at the westerly end of Toronto Island. Over the next few years an amusement park developed in close proximity to the hotel and by the turn of the century was one of the most popular attractions in the entire city. Access to Hanlan's Point Amusement Park, **seen in the above photograph taken on Dominion Day, 1913,** was via one of twelve ferryboats that plied the waters of Toronto Bay. Boats with once-familiar names such as *Trillium* (restored in 1974–75 and returned to service in 1976), *Bluebell, Mayflower, Primrose, John Hanlan* (named for the famous sculler's father and the person for whom Hanlan's Point is named), *Jasmine* and the tiny *Luella*. In addition to a large merry-go-round, a scenic railway, an airplane ride, games emporium, dance hall, and theatre, there was also a large wooden grandstand where lacrosse and baseball games were played. From 1897 until 1900, and then again from 1908 until 1909, the Toronto Maple Leaf baseball team of the International League played their rivals in this stadium. During the 1909 season it burned to the ground, and for the remainder of the season the team moved to Diamond Park on the mainland, just north of the Exhibition grounds. In 1910 a new, larger concrete stadium to be known as Maple Leaf Park

opened, and it was here that a nineteen-year-old pitcher for the Providence Grays knocked a ball right out of the park and into the bay, where it remains to this day. The perpetrator of this (his first professional) home-run – Lorne "Babe" Ruth.

During the first two decades of this century the amusement park thrived. Thousands flocked to Hanlan's Point to ride the amusements, watch the ball games, dance at the pavilion or listen to the Toronto Concert Band play the music of Sousa and Elgar. In 1926, the owners of the ferryboats and amusement park sold their interests to the city. Commencing the following year, all ferry operations were handled by the Toronto Transportation Company. However, with the move of the popular ball team to its new stadium at the foot of Bathurst Street and the much more accessible Sunnyside amusement park on the mainland, the popularity of Hanlan's Point Amusement Park decreased rapidly. Eventually, most of the rides and structures were to be dismantled, and in 1937 an airport was to cover most of the former amusement area.

There was one other factor that contributed to the Island park's demise (a factor that was also to sound the end for Sunnyside almost twenty years later). As one flapper put it, "You can't park a ferryboat on Lover's Lane." The impact of the automobile was starting to be felt.

Hanlan's Point was continually being misspelled, as it is on these two picture postcards. It was named in recognition of John Hanlan, an early settler. His famous son, Ned, always signed his name using two "a"s. The top postcard shows the grand merry-go-round, the lagoon boardwalk, and a portion of the Figure-8 roller-coaster, just visible through the trees. The lower card features the modern (for its day) 18,000-seat Maple Leaf Park stadium that opened in 1910. In the right foreground is an aeroplane ride, a spectacular attraction when one considers that most Torontonians hadn't even seen a real airplane until Count Jacques de Lesseps flew over the city the same year that the stadium opened.

An interesting feature of the Island stadium is revealed by a small sign in the right bottom corner of the postcard declaring that Star Beer was on sale during baseball games. Times change. Beer wasn't available at Blue Jay games (legally) until 1982.

These two postcards are older than those on the preceding page, a fact borne out by the presence in both views of the old wooden grandstand and billboards surrounding the athletic field. The top view also shows the Figure-8 ride which, in fact, was a variation of the traditional wooden roller-coaster. In the distance you can see the rather lacklustre skyline of a city boasting a population of just over 200,000. The bottom view shows an earlier design for the aeroplane ride. In another thirty or so years the new Port George VI Island Airport (now known as Toronto City Centre Airport) would occupy most of the land and lagoons shown in the background of this postcard view.

Shooting the Shoots at Hanlans Point Toronto

Opposite

On the afternoon of August 10, 1909, while bathers were enjoying themselves on this simplified version of a Shoot the Chutes ride (shown in the postcard view top left), a seemingly innocent fire broke out in the Little Gem vaudeville house near the wooden grandstand bleachers. Suddenly that little blaze erupted into an inferno that would ultimately destroy all but five small concession booths at Hanlan's Point Amusement Park. The blaze was discovered at 3:35 pm and less than two hours later more than $200,000 damage had been done. Sadly, a young cashier working at the vaudeville house was burned to death in her wicket. The park was rebuilt in time for the 1910 season.

Above

Following the city's takeover of the ferryboats and amusement park in late 1926, it wasn't long before the city, in turn, put the entire ferryboat fleet and operation of the park into the hands of the recently established Toronto Transportation Commission. Effective April 14, 1927, the TTC added to its fleet of 984 electric streetcars and handful of gasoline buses a total of eight steam-powered ferryboats – *Mayflower, Primrose, Jasmine, John Hanlan, Clark Brothers, Luella, Blue Bell,* and *Trillium* – and a huge amusement park. Initially, the vessels were looked after by staff of the Motor Coach Department until a separate Ferry Department was established two years later. Park operations came under the Commercial (later Public Relations) Department. The TTC ran the park until the latter's demise in the mid-1930s, but kept operating the ferryboats until the service was taken over by the Parks Department of Metropolitan Toronto on January 1, 1962. Many can still remember when a ferryboat ride cost two streetcar tickets.

One of the more popular rides was the Autocar, twice around for a nickel.

Overleaf

Many visitors to the Island crossed the Bay just to dance the night away under the mirror ball. Scores of company and church picnics were held on the old baseball diamond, abandoned when the Maple Leaf team moved to the mainland in 1926.

Above The dance pavilion.

Top right Interior of the dance pavilion.

Bottom right The baseball diamond. Close inspection of the city's skyline reveals (centre) the towering John Street pumphouse chimney, now the site of SkyDome, and to the right of it the clock tower of "old" City Hall, the tallest structure in the city.

On the south side of Queen Street East, between Maclean and Leuty avenues, was Scarboro Beach Park **(above and right),** a popular amusement park that opened for its first season in 1907. Five years later the thirty-seven-acre park was taken over by the Toronto Railway Company, the privately owned streetcar operator in the city. This was a sound business move for the T.R.C., as it enabled the company to utilize its extensive fleet of street railway equipment during non-rush hour periods and on weekends. The park itself consisted of a lovely picnic grove, a lacrosse stadium/bicycle track, and an extensive collection of popular amusement rides and games. In the centre of the park was a 100-foot-high tower with a powerful beacon on top. The tower was outlined with small lights and the beacon itself could be seen for miles. One of the most popular rides was the Shoot the Chutes. Passengers boarded the little boats, were hauled up an incline to a height of approximately seventy-five feet, the boats were rotated, and then sent plummeting down the chutes into a large pond of water. When the boats hit the water they would slow to a stop in an enormous shower of water that would soak passengers and spectators alike. Scarboro Beach Park also had an aeroplane ride, which in itself is interesting since it was at this park on September 7, 1909, that Charles Willard performed one of North America's first air shows in his *Golden Flyer* Curtis biplane. The newspapers of the day were unimpressed. Typical headlines read "Airship went up, airship came down" and "Willard's plane prefers the water," the latter headline prompted by the pilot's habit of putting his craft down in Lake Ontario when curious spectators congregated on his landing strip along the sandy beach.

Goin' up.

Comin' down.

Scarboro Beach Opening

Saturday, May 20th, 1922

AFTERNOON	EVENING
CHILDREN'S COSTUME PARADE AND CONTEST. BALLOON ASCENSION. VAUDEVILLE DANCING IMPERIAL CONCERT BAND. RADIO REPORT.	ADULT'S COSTUME PARADE AND CONTEST. VAUDEVILLE GAMES DANCING ORCHESTRA IMPERIAL CONCERT BAND. RADIO REPORT.

A CARNIVAL OF FUN FOR YOUNG AND OLD

Do not fail to come to Scarboro' Beach Park on Opening Day. The two costume parades and carnival will open the summer season. Hundreds of prizes for Fancy, Funny and Crazy Costumes. Everyone has a chance. The Park will be the brightest spot in Ontario on that day, with Band Concert, Vaudeville, Moving Pictures, Dancing Pavilion, New Games, Shoot the Chutes, Figure 3, Old Mill, etc. The first open air Radio Report will be inaugurated on Opening Day with Speeches, Recitation, Song.

Join the happy throng. Come and enjoy yourself. Take in this 3-in-1 Gala Day. Concerts, Masquerade and Parade all in one.

FUN! LAUGHS! MIRTH! PLEASURE! AMUSEMENT! PRIZES!

Prizes Include Square Grand Piano, Organ, Gramophone

The Scenic Railway **(top)** was a favourite ride with visitors to Scarboro Beach Park. Nearby was a carousel that it is believed was eventually shipped across the lake to Lakeside Park outside Port Dalhousie (now a suburb of St. Catharines) where the ride still operates. The speed of the Lakeside Park carousel is still regulated by an old streetcar controller, a fact that helps confirm the theory that the carousel came from the Toronto Railway Company's park. Just out of view to the left was an entrance gate that straddled a sandy path leading south into the park from Queen Street. Today, this path is Scarborough Beach Boulevard.

Visible in the lower photo are the shooting gallery, hoop game, red-hot stand, and circus gallery. In front of them was a large open-air stage where trapeze artists, acrobats, jugglers, and magicians entertained visitors to the park. Beside the stage was a bandstand where D'Urbano's Band would play stirring martial airs, or Maggie Barr, "the Queen of Scottish Song," would give forth with a "voice of liquid sweetness." A local paper once wrote of Maggie:

Welcome! O'Scottish song of the star;
Liltin' at will o'love or war;
Welcome once mair, sweet Maggie Barr.

Another favourite spectator sport at the park was the six-day bicycle race held on the dirt track inside the lacrosse stadium. A frequent participant in these races, as well as others around the continent, was William "Torchy" Peden – "Torchy" for his shock of red hair. Peden was a Victoria, B.C., native who took to bicycle racing at an early age and eventually became the country's most famous six-day race participant. These races became as popular as today's Stanley Cup, World Series, or Grey Cup play-offs. Perhaps a brief description of just what a six-day bike race was all about will help explain the event's popularity. A six-day race meant exactly that, the race lasted 144 hours with cyclists pedalling around and around a track stopping only briefly for food and drink. This type of human endurance contest was first run in 1891 and by 1898 was considered so cruel that the state of New York decreed that no participant in such a race could pedal for more than twelve hours in one twenty-four hour period. The cyclists' answer to this ruling, seemingly designed to take away the crowds' desire to see the cyclists drop, was to form teams so that the race could continue at the same stomach-churning pace as before. An added thrill resulted when, on signal, the fastest participants would take to the track and a contest to claim the lead position would ensue. With alarming frequency, several competing cyclists would bump together and end up in a pile against the fence. Three times in succession "Torchy" and his partner (another Canadian, Fred Spencer) captured the six-day marathon championship at New York City's Madison Square Gardens. Hard as it may be to believe, in November 1931, twenty-five-year-old "Torchy" set the world's cycle speed record for the paced mile at an incredible seventy-four miles per hour.

Outings to the Scarboro Beach Park ended abruptly in 1925 when officials of the Toronto Railway Company locked the gates to its property. The company attempted to force the business on the new Toronto Transportation Commission, but the TTC fought that idea. The Commission's mandate was to provide the public with an efficient transportation system, not an amusement park. Eventually the property was sold to the Provident Investment Company after which the land was cleared of all buildings and rides. Soon dozens of new houses began to appear on the site of what was one of Toronto's most popular amusement parks.

In addition to the parks just described, there were several others just a boat or boat-and-streetcar ride away. Parks such as Crystal Beach (on Lake Erie), Lorne Park (on Lake Ontario just west of Toronto), Grimsby Beach (between St. Catharines and Hamilton on Lake Ontario), and Lakeside Park (also on Lake Ontario near the mouth of the Welland Canal) welcomed hundreds of thousands of happy visitors every summer. The latter park, which was opened in 1902 and over its lifetime was served by a multitude of lake steamers, was actually located in Port Dalhousie, a small community that became part of St. Catharines, Ontario, in 1961. From Lakeside Park high-speed electric streetcars ran to and from the nearby cities of St. Catharines and Niagara Falls, Ontario and New York, making the park a perfect place for a day or weekend outing.

For most of its existence, Lakeside Park was owned and operated by the Niagara, St. Catharines, and Toronto Navigation Company, a transit-oriented concern that operated two of the most famous lake steamers to run out of Toronto. *Dalhousie City* was built in Collingwood, Ontario, in 1911 and was the mainstay of the Toronto–Port Dalhousie service until 1949, when she was sold to Inland Lines Limited of Montreal. Renamed *Island King II* she was destroyed by fire at Lachine, Quebec, in November 1960. Her running mate was the strikingly beautiful *Northumberland*, a vessel that entered service on Lake Ontario in 1920 after operating for many years from ports in England and then between Prince Edward Island and the Canadian mainland. Built in 1891, *Northumberland* came to a tragic end when she was destroyed by fire at her berth at Lakeside Park on June 22, 1949, just three months before the infamous *Noronic* fire at Toronto's Pier 9, the latter still our city's greatest disaster.

Lakeside Park was eventually sold to the park's manager, who, in turn, relinquished ownership to the City of St. Catharines.

Bathers can still soak up the sun on Lakeside's sandy beaches or take a spin on the old carousel. Somehow, though, it's just not the same.

Above

They say that getting there's half the fun and if the expressions on the faces of those in this photo are any indication "they" must be right. Electric streetcars were introduced to Torontonians on August 15th, 1892, and immediately became a popular way of getting to and from pleasure parks such as Scarboro Beach Park and Munro Park. The latter was a small picnic grove complete with swings, a round-about, and a 14,000-square-foot dance pavilion. Details of Munro Park are sketchy at best, although it is recorded that the twenty-six-acre park was owned at one time by the Toronto Railway Company, and that the company's new electric streetcars on the *King* route ran there as early as 1898. In fact, it may be that the well-dressed crowd in the photograph is boarding the *King* car and trailer at the Munro Park terminal for a return trip to the city. Interestingly, the trailer shown here, #192, was built the same year that the first electric streetcars in the city ran on Church Street. This vehicle was one of 169 lost in the sensational King East Division carhouse fire on December 28, 1916. A portion of this old carhouse remains, forming the north wall of the structure at the southeast corner of King and St. Lawrence streets, just west of the Don River.

John Howard's Sunnyside Villa is seen in the foreground
with the hulking Sacred Heart Orphanage in behind.
When the larger building was converted into the new St.
Joseph's Hospital in 1921 a number of doctors moved their
offices into the old Sunnyside Villa which was eventually
demolished and the present parking garage erected on
the site in 1977.

TWO
John George Howard's Sunnyside

When Sunnyside Bathing Pavilion and Amusement Park opened on the shores of Humber Bay in the spring of 1922, the use of the term "Sunnyside" to describe the location of the city's new "playground by the Lake" had, in fact, described this locale for almost three-quarters of a century. The first recorded use of the term occurs when John George Howard, who's property encompassed much of today's High Park, constructed a summer villa many miles west of the city. His "Sunnyside Villa," as the Warden of High Park called the small structure, was located on the sunny side of a hill just north of the present busy Queensway, approximately midway between Glendale and Sunnyside avenues. In those days the Lake Ontario shoreline was not much further south than where The Queensway was to be built in the mid-1950s. With this information it's easy to understand how a fine residence perched on the sunny side of a grassy hill, remote from any other large structures save for Howard's permanent residence, Colborne Lodge, which was (and still is) located some distance to the west, would lend its name to the immediate vicinity. In fact, the Sunnyside area was never fully defined in terms of strict boundaries other than the lake, which was the southernmost boundary. Eventually, Roncesvalles Avenue and the Humber River became the rather arbitrary east and west boundaries of the Sunnyside district with an undefined line north of the old Lake Shore Road as the northern limit.

It wasn't until January 2, 1888, that, in official terms at least, an area called Sunnyside, comprising a total of 115.2 acres and located north of what had been the traditional Sunnyside, was annexed to the city. It was on this same date that Seaton Village (the area north and west of the Bloor and Bathurst intersection), Rathnally (a small area on the west side of Avenue Road, just north of the *CPR* tracks), and North Yorkville were also added to the fast-growing City of Toronto.

In 1876, John Howard's former summer residence became part of the new Sisters of St. Joseph's Sacred Heart Orphanage. Over the next few years the area became more and more populated and in 1889 the nearby Town of Parkdale, with its 4,583 citizens, joined the city as St. Alban's Ward. This annexation extended the city's western boundary to Roncesvalles Avenue. Four years later, on May 27, 1893, a long ribbon of land comprising twelve acres stretching from Roncesvalles Avenue to the Humber River and taking in all the land from a point north of the old Lake Shore Road down to the water's edge also became part of the city. Finally, Sunnyside, as it was known to Howard's generation, was officially part of Toronto.

| Humber Bay | Fort Rouille (at the foot of the present-day Dufferin Street) | Fort York | Town of York (at east end of the Bay) | Toronto Island (at this time still a peninsula) |

Above

Some thirty-five years before John George Howard built his villa, the area had been witness to a large influx of Americans, although this time they were hardly here for a friendly visit. In fact, they were here to do battle, and by the time the gun smoke and dust had settled, the Town of York was under the flag of the United States of America. It all started on June 18, 1812, when antagonism between Britain and the United States erupted into all-out war, known to every Canadian school child (I hope) as the War of 1812. American politicians believed that the capture of British North America (Upper and Lower Canada) could be accomplished by "a few companies of Kentucky and Tennessee riflemen." One of the key targets in this project was the little capital of Upper Canada, a town called York (now Toronto) with a total population of 625 and believed to be "easy pickings."

On the morning of April 25, 1813, the American commander, Major-General Henry Dearborn, dispatched his invasion force of 1,750 men from Sackett's Harbour at the east end of Lake Ontario. Sailing up the lake in fourteen vessels mounting a total of eighty-three guns and manned by 700 officers and ratings, the armada arrived off the tip of the Peninsula (now Toronto Island) the following day. The enemy was spotted and the alarm given. As April 27 dawned, a stiff easterly wind sprang up and forced the ships to the west and the invaders eventually came ashore near the foot of present-day Roncesvalles Avenue. Here they were met by a small party of native people under Major James Givins' command and members of the Grenadier Company of the 8th Regiment led by Captain McNeale. The defenders were overwhelmed, and within two hours the invaders were advancing from the Sunnyside area toward Fort York. It was during this retreat that several of the Grenadiers fell through the melting ice covering a body of water now known as Grenadier Pond in tribute to those valiant defenders of York. Subsequent skirmishes preceded the eventual capitulation of the capital, but not before more than 300 of the invaders had

been killed, including explorer/soldier Zebulon Pike, for whom the mountain peak in Colorado is named. For six days our community was, for all intents and purposes, an American town with invading troops roaming the streets at will, albeit under close check by their military leaders. When the Americans finally left the town on May 2 they took with them the mace, the symbol of legislative authority, books from the public subscription library (located in Elmsley House at the corner of King and Simcoe streets), as well as the Royal Standard. There are several interesting sidelights to the brief occupation. The first has to do with the Americans' belief that the mace had a human scalp tied to it. In fact, the scalp was nothing more than the clerk's powdered wig. A second suggests that the term White House was first used after the President's mansion was whitewashed to conceal the damage inflicted by fire during the British attack on Washington on August 24, 1814. A British general recorded in his diary that the attack on the American capital, and the President's mansion in particular, was done in retaliation for the attack on the capital of the Province of Upper Canada.

Known as the "Warden of High Park," John George Howard was born in Bengeo, Hertfordshire, England, in 1803, and at the age of fifteen he went to sea. After a couple of years the young man gave up his desire to become a sailor and, once back on dry land, began studying land surveying, engineering, and architecture. In 1832, Howard and his wife, Jemima, arrived in Canada and settled in the little Town of York where the population was approaching 5,500 enterprising souls. The following year, Sir John Colborne, lieutenant-governor of Upper Canada and founder of Upper Canada College, obtained for Howard the position of drawing master at the college. In 1843, nine years after York had been given city status and renamed Toronto, Howard was made City Surveyor. The next year Howard, along with Frederick Barron, the principal of Upper Canada College, purchased from George Cruickshank (for £750, approximately $3,750) 160 acres of land that abutted Howard's original 165-acre parcel of land that he had acquired just four years after his arrival in York in 1832. Howard had called his proposed "sheep farm" High Park and erected a dwelling on it which he named after his benefactor. In 1873, John Howard deeded his sprawling estate, including his house, to the citizens of Toronto. Colborne Lodge still stands as a reminder of Howard's extraordinary benevolence.

Howard eventually purchased Barron's interest in the new parcel of land with a view to subdividing the property and selling building lots. Instead, in 1848 he erected a summer residence at the southeast corner of the property which he sold to George Cheney, a stove manufacturer, five years later. Unfortunately, Cheney defaulted on the mortgage and four years later Howard was to sell the villa again, this time to a Mr. Paterson. History is vague on the following few years, but what is known is that by 1876 the property had come into the possession of Henry Speid. Weeks prior to returning to his birthplace in Scotland, Speid visited various charities in Toronto and decided to loan his estate to the Children's Department of the House of Providence on Power Street. In 1891, following the five-year loan period, Speid sold Sunnyside to the Roman Catholic diocese for $9,500 and it became a branch of the House of Providence known as Sacred Heart Orphanage. In 1920, the city sought to expropriate the orphanage which by this time had grown in size but still included Howard's original villa. The Sisters acted quickly and sent some of the children to the R.J. Fleming estate at the northeast corner of St. Clair Avenue and Bathurst Street. They then

John George Howard (1803–1890), the Warden of High Park.

converted part of the orphanage into a hospital which, according to the laws of the day, could not be expropriated. St. Joseph's Hospital was born.

As an aside, there are two theories as to how the name Sunnyside came about. The first suggests that John George Howard penned the term simply because his summer villa was located on the sunny side of a hill. A more interesting, yet unconfirmed, possibility is that the subsequent owner of the villa, George Cheney, came up with the name to honour his favourite American author, Washington Irving (1783–1859), who wrote many of his short stories, including "Rip Van Winkle," "Bracebridge Hall," and "Tales of a Traveller" at his North Tarrytown, New York, estate that he called Sunnyside.

Opposite

This map is taken from the *Illustrated Historical Atlas of York County* published in 1878. Indian Road, originally an ancient Indian footpath, is seen running through Lot 35 in the First Concession from the bay. It was on parcels 13, 14, and 15 (unnumbered on this map) of Lot 36 that Howard built Sunnyside Villa in 1848. Over the years the villa was remodelled and it eventually became part of Sacred Heart Orphanage then St. Joseph's Hospital. The historic structure was unceremoniously demolished in 1945. As can be seen on the map, several prominent local citizens had large estates and eventually gave their surnames to thoroughfares in the Town of Parkdale that became simply St. Alban's Ward after annexation by the city in 1889. Examples of these streets are those named for Col. A.R. Dunn (Dunn Avenue) and Dr. William Gwynne (Gwynne Avenue). Note also John Ellis in Swansea, whose name lives on with Ellis Avenue. Other prominent citizens after whom local thoroughfares have been named and also found on this map: Charles Keele, John and Edward Scarlett, Francis Silverthorn, Patrick Lappen [*sic*], David Kennedy, and so forth.

Above

The Sunnyside area of Toronto was the site of a daring rescue performed by Thomas Tinning, a citizen of the city who in his seventy-two years performed numerous such rescues. The event depicted in this painting by John George Howard (whose residence, Colborne Lodge, can be seen on the hill to the left) occurred one stormy morning in December 1861. It was Howard who saw the schooner *Pacific* foundering in Humber Bay and, rushing into the city, alerted Thomas Tinning. Tinning returned to the scene with Howard, a volunteer crew, and a lifeboat from the steamer *Zimmerman*. The rescuers were capsized several times but they persisted in their attempt, and after a mighty struggle all on board *Pacific* were saved from certain drowning.

Twenty-three years later, this area was again visited by disaster, this time thirty-two times more dreadful. Early in the morning of January 2, 1884, a trainload of workers on their way to the Dominion Bolt and Iron Company, near the foot of today's Windermere Avenue in Swansea, collided head-on with a Toronto-bound Grand Trunk freight train just west of Sunnyside with a resultant loss of thirty-two lives. In those days, there was but a single track skirting Humber Bay, and between this track and the water's edge was a colonnade of huge Balm of Gilead trees. As the freight cleared the Humber bridge it rounded the edge of the bay and began to pick up speed in order to climb the steep grade into Parkdale, a grade that was eliminated during the massive Parkdale Grade Separation project carried out in the early 1900s. On that blind curve the freight met the commuter train with a deafening crash. Due to the poor communication procedures of the time, news of the disaster and subsequent rescue attempts were delayed adding greatly to the scope of the tragedy.

Opposite

These two photos were taken ninety-three years apart from the same vantage point at King Street West and Wilson (now Wilson Park) Road. The 1887 view shows the Humber Bay flanked by a wooden fence and the single track of the Grand Trunk Railway. It was in this area of Sunnyside that the head-on collision of the ill-fated trains occurred on January 2, 1884.

In the distance, just inland from the maximum indentation of the bay, one can see the old Parkdale pumping station, next to which was a toll-gate run by a man named Everleigh. To the extreme right we see the white cupola of the Ocean House Hotel. This building, erected in 1884 by Thomas Scholes, still stands (*sans* cupola) at the southeast corner of Roncesvalles Avenue and Queen Street West.

In the foreground is an outbuilding, probably a stable belonging to John Beaty, an official at the Customs House in downtown Toronto. Beaty bought the land between Dowling and Roncesvalles south of Queen Street for $200 per acre in 1872. Beaty Avenue is named for this resident, while Triller Avenue commemorates his wife's maiden name.

The present day (1980) **(bottom)** photo, taken from approximately the same point as the 1887 view, shows the almost unbelievable changes that have occurred in the past ninety-three years. In that space of time, Sunnyside Amusement Park, the subject of this book, has come and gone.

Above

In this photograph taken by William James early this century on the shore of the old Humber Bay at Sunnyside we see a couple of intrepid young fishermen closely scrutinizing the work of talented Toronto artist Owen Staples. Staples had joined the staff of the *Evening Telegram* newspaper in 1885 as a reporter-illustrator. At that time only hand-drawn illustrations were being used to supplement news stories. The technology needed to reproduce photographic images was still many years in the future. Staples also prepared most of the sketches that where used to illustrate the remarkable "Landmarks of Toronto" columns that were a favourite of John Ross Robertson, founder and publisher of the *Evening Telegram* newspaper and appeared in the paper for many years around the turn of the century. During the period 1894–1914 these columns, complete with Staples' illustrations, were published in six volumes with each volume selling for two dollars. Today, the set of "Landmarks of Toronto" frequently fetches in excess of $1,000.

Staples remained with the paper for almost sixty years and today many of his paintings are in the Metro Toronto Library and City of Toronto collections.

*Sunnyside
at turn
Century*

Above

A favourite pastime of Torontonians at the turn of the
century was a leisurely walk along the boardwalk at Sunnyside. In this view, looking east along the old Lake Shore
Road near the foot of today's Parkside Drive, the horse-
drawn carriage is seen bound for Mimico, just across the
bridge over the Humber River. Mimico is an Indian word
said to mean "home of wild pigeons." On the south side of
Lake Shore Road is the dining establishment of Mrs.
Pauline Meyer, a former hairdresser who opened this
large restaurant on the waterfront and it soon became a
favourite place for fish dinners and ice-cream sodas.

Above

An absolutely delightful photograph by a marvellous Toronto photographer, William James, captures a moment in time for all time. To the left, a jauntily clad beau puts the hustle on a young belle, much to the outrage of the prim and proper group seated to the right. One young lady just can't believe what she's just witnessed. (Did he pinch her? Did she enjoy it?) This candid action photo was taken early this century on the old Lake Shore Road, just south of High Park. Mrs. Meyer's dining establishment can be seen along the shoreline in the centre distance.

Above

Formed on November 14, 1890, the Toronto & Mimico Electric Railway & Light Company was empowered "to build and operate a street railway on Lake Shore Road west from Toronto and to sell electric power to customers along the route." Progress on building the streetcar line was slow with part of the project, the stretch from the junction of the old Lake Shore Road and Queen Street at the steam railway crossing west to the Humber River, finally opening in the summer of 1892. At this time the line operated infrequently during the winter months and was almost exclusively a summer sightseeing route. To protect horses the following rule was established by the County of York:

> In case the electric motors or cars used by the Company, their successors or assign, in operating the said road while passing along the said railway or tramway shall cause alarm to any horse travelling or being upon the said roadway with

vehicle or otherwise, the motor or cars of the company shall, if necessary, be stopped to enable the horses so alarmed to pass. The servants of the said company shall assist the person or persons riding or driving or in charge of the horse or horses that may be alarmed as aforesaid so as to prevent accident or injury to the person or persons, horse or horses, upon said roadway. So far as safely can be done without causing alarm or injury to horses or vehicles upon the said roadway the speed of the cars may not exceed at any time 12 miles per hour.

On July 1, 1893, the Toronto Railway Company, which ran the city streetcars, took over operations and nine days later extended the service westerly three-quarters of a mile west of the Humber to Mimico Creek. Then, a year later, the company completed a further extension to Long Branch. Cars in operation on this line included double-deck cars, #10 and #11 (**seen above on the old Lake**

Shore Road at Sunnyside); two converted horse cars, #30 and #188, and a former trailer, #201, which was subsequently rebuilt into an electric-motor streetcar. As more and more summer cottages were built along the lakefront, newer and larger vehicles were required and on June 20, 1896, #1 and #3 **(shown above)** were introduced. These cars, which seated ninety-six people, were originally designed as double deckers but were remodelled and became the pride of the Mimico line.

In the photo the cars are seen in front of the Sacred Heart Orphanage which at the time was using Howard's old Sunnyside Villa to house the administrative offices. The old structure can be seen as the white structure just to the right of centre in the photo. Towns scattered along the street railway route, such as Mimico, New Toronto, and Long Branch, continued to grow and by 1905 the line had been extended to Port Credit with the ultimate intention of extending service to Hamilton and Niagara Falls. One year earlier the owners of the line, the Toronto Railway Company, merged this route with its other two suburban lines, the Scarboro (east city limits to West Hill) and Metropolitan (north city limits to Lake Simcoe), thereby creating the Toronto and York Radial Railway Company. In 1922, the three suburban lines were acquired by the city with the operation of the Scarboro and Port Credit lines turned over to the Hydro Electric Power Commission of Ontario (now simply Ontario

Hydro). Operation of these lines was transferred to the TTC in 1928. Streetcar service to Port Credit ended seven years later. The Long Branch portion (to Brown's Line) continues as part of the 501 (*Queen*) route.

Above

Taken by an anonymous amateur photographer around the turn of the century, this photograph shows the Sunnyside area at the foot of Indian Road. To the left, we can see a portion of the old boardwalk, a section of Lake Shore Road, the Mimico radial tracks, and, up on the embankment, the tracks of the Grand Trunk Railway. The white railway-crossing gate protects the Indian Road crossing over the steam tracks. Today the area is buried beneath the underpasses and embankments that make up the Gardiner Expressway/Parkside Drive/railway right-of-way agglomeration.

Above

As a result of the Parkdale Grade Separation, which was designed to ease the job faced by toiling steam engines as they climbed and the long gradient between the Humber River and the railway's freight and passenger yards in the downtown part of the city, the Queen / King / Roncesvalles intersection was isolated from Lake Shore Road. In 1912, the railway company was forced to build a traffic bridge connecting that intersection with the old Lake Shore Road running westerly to Port Credit, Oakville, and Hamilton. The construction of that bridge resulted in the demolition of the old Parkdale pumping station, a favourite locale for public swimming. On July 8, 1914, residents of the area asked the Harbour Commission to establish a new bathing station on the beach. The commissioners awarded Mr. Emil Brooker the right to build a bath house on the beach just east of the bridge shown here and to charge for bathing privileges. In deference to those who couldn't afford the luxury of paying to swim, the City established a free bathing beach just west of Mr. Brooker's operation. The free bathing beach, including its water slide, participants, and spectators, is shown in this view.

Emil Brooker and his wife, known as Ma and Pa Brooker, later opened one of the city's first drive-in restaurants just west of the Humber River on the south side of Lake Shore Road.

Top Panorama Looking west along the old Lake Shore Road we see the single track of the Mimico radial street-car line and the mainline of the Grand Trunk Railway as they appeared at the turn of the century. The multitude of trees in the background is located on the three properties of Messrs. Howard, Chapman, and Ridout, those 400 acres now known, collectively, as High Park.

The dirt path that crosses the tracks and terminates in a small boat ramp became Indian Road, a thoroughfare that comes by its name honestly as it actually follows an old Indian trail. To the extreme right is the factory of the former MacDonell Rolling Mills Company that became the Toronto Bolt & Forging Company in 1903. In 1910, this operation changed names again this time to the Canada Bolt and Nut Company Limited. Soon after it became part of the Steel Company of Canada Limited. This latter enterprise was established on June 9, 1910, by combining the assets of the Hamilton Steel & Iron Company Limit-

ed, Montreal Rolling Mills Company, Canada Screw Company Limited, Dominion Wire Manufacturing Company Limited, and Canada Bolt and Nut Company Limited. Several years later the inefficient Lake Shore Road plant seen in the photo was closed down and operations moved a short distance to the west to Stelco's Swansea Works. This factory had its origins back in 1882 when John Livingston opened a 40,000-square-foot plant on Windermere Avenue known as the Dominion Bolt Works.

The old Lake Shore Road, the radial and railway tracks, and the rolling mill depicted in the panoramic photograph are now buried deep beneath the Gardiner Expressway.

The photo at the **bottom of the opposite page** was taken *circa* 1902 and shows youngsters enjoying a sum-

mer outing in a partly submerged canoe at the public bathing beach near the foot of Roncesvalles Avenue. In the **above photo** the view is looking west along the Grand Trunk right of way at the Queen Street West crossing. Buildings to the left are on Lake Shore Road, the continuation of Queen Street running south and west from the crossing. Just to the right of the police officer in the white summer bobby helmet we catch a glimpse of Mrs. Meyer's restaurant.

A promotion sponsored by the *Evening Telegram* newspaper drew thousands to the Sunnyside Bathing Pavilion on August 23, 1923. Billed as a "Water Nymph Carnival" the event was "to encourage girls and young women in the art of swimming."

Three

The Birth of Sunnyside Amusement Park

The Sunnyside Bathing Pavilion and Amusement Park were the direct result of a plan formulated by the newly established Toronto Harbour Commission. For many years prior to 1912 control of the City's waterfront, from the Humber River on the west to the foot of Victoria Park Avenue on the east, was in the hands of various agencies and private individuals. The results were often chaotic. Finally, on May 19, 1911, the citizens approved the passage of the Toronto Harbour Commissioners Act. In July of the following year five Commissioners were appointed and the new Toronto Harbour Commission was in business. On November 2 of that same year, City Council authorized by Order-in-Council P.C. 1426 that a complete set of plans for the redevelopment of the waterfront be prepared by the new Commission and submitted to the federal Department of Public Works for its approval and, hopefully, funding.

In addition to major physical changes to the Central and Eastern Harbour Terminal areas, changes that ultimately included over 1,400 acres of land reclamation, construction of new wharves, and the deepening of the harbour to twenty-four feet to permit access by vessels using the proposed New Welland Canal (which would not open until 1932), the plan called for the development of recreational facilities and parkland along the waterfront strip from just west of Bathurst Street to the Humber River. To protect this Western Section development, a new four-mile-long breakwall was also to be constructed. Having received all necessary approvals, work on the massive waterfront project, the total cost of which was estimated at $19 million, began in 1913. Work was slowed by the outbreak of the First World War, but continued at a quickened pace following cessation of hostilities. By the end of 1922, the year the Pavilion and Amusement Park opened, almost seventy-five percent of the immense Western Section project had been completed.

When the dust had settled several years later some 330 acres had been developed by the Harbour Commission. That total included 113 acres of protected waterways behind 17,985 lineal feet of breakwall, 115 acres of parklands, and 86 acres of industrial land which was offered for sale or lease. In addition, there were 16 acres of dedicated streets, including the new Lakeshore Boulevard and Lake Shore Road that were laid out on land created by pumping more than 4,000,000 cubic yards of sandy muck from the lake bottom and distributing it along a four-mile stretch of the western waterfront shoreline.

The idea of having an amusement park in the Humber Bay area can be attributed to one Charles Phillips who, as far back as 1911, offered the newly organized Toronto Harbour Commission $2,000 per annum to permit him to operate a single amusement device on the shore of the old Humber Bay. Nothing ever came of this early request, but as the development of the new Sunnyside Amusement Park proceeded, the Commission was continually deluged with requests from citizens to operate various lakeside amusement park concessions, such as beach chair rentals, palmistry tents, a Liberty Root Beer stand, a rotisserie restaurant, an open-air theatre, souvenir stands, guess-your-weight scales, a drug store, a char-à-banc sightseeing service, a cleaning, pressing, and shoe-shine shop, various amusement rides, a kosher delicatessen, and, from an enquirer in Philadelphia, Pennsylvania, a request to operate a wheel chair concession. After weeding through dozens and dozens of requests the Toronto Harbour Commission, the landlord of the new park, approved the installation of seven rides, including an Aero Swing and two other low-level swings, Frolic and Dodgem rides, a merry-go-round (all operated by the Sunnyside Amusement Company), and a Whip (operated by J.B. Atkinson). Also approved were nine games of skill (Monkey Racer, Coney Racer, a shooting gallery (all operated by J.R. McIntyre), a bowling alley, fish pond, Kentucky Derby, Torpedo Race, balloon race, and Figure 8 (operated by the Sunnyside Amusement Company), ten refreshment stands (two to be operated by "Cap" Burk, five by the Sunnyside Amusement Company, and one each by the Sunnyside Service Company, F. & D. Ryan, and the Palais Royale Limited), and seven miscellaneous attractions, including boat rentals at the Palais Royale, W. Mitchell's silhouette stand, Jeck's Boats (over on the Humber River), George Deller's pair of Guess-Your-Weight stands, Fred Williams' beach chair concession, and some high-powered telescopes operated by someone named DeWitt.

The bathing pavilion across the south side of Lakeshore Boulevard did a landslide business that first year and Sunnyside soon gained the title of "the playground by the lake." And on a warm summer evening Sunnyside became "the city of lights" and Toronto's newest place to be and to be seen.

Lynn Beach, Massachusetts.

Above

A quick look at this photo might lead readers to believe that it's a view of the present Sunnyside Bathing Pavilion. However, a closer look reveals that this is, in fact, some other facility. When the Toronto Harbour Commission agreed to construct a bathing establishment on the western waterfront, Edward Cousins, the Commission's industrious general manager and chief engineer, visited various North American cities to get some ideas for the new facility to be erected at Sunnyside. It was the structure pictured here, the bathing pavilion at Lynn Beach, Massachusetts, that caught his eye and that of the architect Alfred Chapman who then designed our Sunnyside Bathing Pavilion. Chapman has numerous other creations in the Toronto area, including the Ontario Government Building, the Princes' Gates in the Canadian National Exhibition grounds, and Havergal College on Avenue Road.

Opposite

During the creation of the new Sunnyside bathing beach in 1921, it became necessary to find a plentiful supply of top soil and sod to dress the newly reclaimed land. To ensure itself of a plentiful source of rich soil, the Harbour Commission purchased a ninety-six-acre farm in Pickering Township owned by David Annin. A railway siding was laid into the property and special rail cars shunted into place, loaded with top soil and hauled to a depot near Sunnyside. Dump trucks made the final delivery to the waterfront where a new beach was created. In total, 40,000 cubic yards were transferred from Pickering to the site of the new beach. Its usefulness fulfilled, the farm was resold by the Harbour Commission. Today, the southern portion of the former Annin property is still farmed while the northern section is held by a developer for future industrial use. Highway 401 touches the most northerly edge of the farm.

Pickering above and Sunnyside below.

OFFICIAL OPENING OF
SUNNYSIDE BEACH
"TORONTO'S LAKESHORE PLAYGROUND"
BY
HIS WORSHIP MAYOR MAGUIRE
AT 6 P.M. ON
WEDNESDAY, JUNE 28
1922
OPENING CEREMONIES AT BATHING PAVILION
Band Concerts---Afternoon and Evening
THE PUBLIC ARE INVITED TO INSPECT THE BUILDING FROM 6 TO 9 P.M.
Bathing After 9 p.m.
48TH HIGHLANDERS, ROYAL GRENADIERS AND QUEEN'S OWN BANDS.
AMUSEMENT DEVICES AND GAMES
SUPERVISED BATHING FACILITIES.   CANOEING AND BOATING
TERRACED TEA GARDENS AND DANCING
LAKEFRONT PROMENADE AND BOULEVARD DRIVE
TWENTY-FIVE MINUTES BY KING STREET CAR FROM KING AND YONGE.
FIFTEEN MINUTES BY AUTOMOBILE

Accolades, boasts, and predictions flowed at a banquet held following the formal opening of Sunnyside Beach and Bathing Pavilion on June 28, 1922:

Toronto is upon the eve of the greatest development in its history. I am quite sure if we try to rise to it we will be in reality – what is only now in promise – a truly great city.
R. Home Smith, Chairman, Toronto Harbour Commission

This city is making wonderful strides. I believe we are at the dawn of the greatest day in its existence.
Sir Adam Beck, Chairman, Hydro-Electric Power Commission of Ontario

The future of Toronto is indeed bright. When future generations see this splendid development and enjoy its privileges they must declare that the men who conceived it had vision. For all time, Toronto will be indebted to the unselfish patriotism of the men who have given of their time and genius to the execution of this work.
Alfred Maguire, Mayor of Toronto

The building is in exceedingly good taste. I feel they have got something in the way of a dream of Palm Beach with the colouring of Ostend blend-ed into a very harmonious Canadian whole. We women who are particularly interested in recreation, as well as all who are anxious to promote health and wholesome recreation for our young people, applaud the conception and fulfilment of such a wonderful institution.
Mrs. Ethel Small, City Alderman for Ward 4 and Chairman of the Parks Committee

The city's newspapers joined the chorus of chest-thumpers with headlines such as:

Sunnyside Inspires Visions of Greatness-to-be of Toronto.
Evening Telegram

Beautiful Sunnyside Beach, Front Doorway of Toronto, is Officially Thrown Open.
Star

Sunnyside Ushers Toronto the Threshold of her New Era.
The *Globe*

Above

Posing for the photographer are the five officials who participated in the June 28, 1922, official opening ceremonies. R. Home Smith *(left)*, a member of the Toronto Harbour Commission from its establishment in 1911 and its chairman in 1921 and 1922. Smith, who was born in Stratford on July 12, 1877, is generally given credit for the Toronto waterfront redevelopment plan of 1912, including his pet project, Sunnyside. Other R. Home Smith projects include the Old Mill Tea Garden (1914) and administration building (1928), and the development of the Baby Point and Kingsway Park real estate subdivisions. In total, Home Smith developed some 3,000 acres along the banks of the Humber River. Smith even proposed the construction of a streetcar line to serve his developments. The line would run from Sunnyside, along the lakeshore, curve north following the route of the present South Kingsway to Bloor Street, then west to the Kingsway and north to Dundas Street. A second line would connect with the first just south of Dundas Street and run in an easterly direction, over the Humber River, to connect with the street railway line on Yonge Street just south of St. Clair Avenue. Neither route was built.

A list of some of the companies and foundations of which Home Smith was president or director corroborates this Torontonian's influence: Mexico Northwestern Railway, Buffalo, Rochester, and Lockport Railway, Algoma Central & Hudson Bay Railway, Algoma Steel Corporation, El Paso Milling Co., Madera Lumber Company, and the Niagara Parks Commission. Home Smith died on February 4, 1935. Alfred Maguire *(second from left)* was a city alderman for thirteen years and Mayor of Toronto for two years, 1922, and 1923. Ethel Small *(centre)* was a member of the 1922 Parks and Exhibitions Committee, Alderman for Ward 4 for three years and only the second female alderman to be elected in the city's history. Edward Lancelot Cousins *(second from right)* was born in Toronto in 1883 and served as the chief engineer of the Toronto Harbour Commission from its inception in 1911 until 1922, and was responsible for the physical redevelopment of Toronto's waterfront from the Humber River to Ashbridges Bay. Tommy Church *(right)* was one of this city's most popular mayors, holding that office from 1915 to 1921, having entered the wonderful world of municipal politics in 1898. After leaving city government, Church entered federal politics as a Member of Parliament. Here he remained until his death in 1950. During the long years of the Great War, Tommy was known as the "soldier's friend," being familiar with hundreds of them on a first-name basis.

Above

Thousands gathered in front of the new Sunnyside Bathing Pavilion to witness the official opening ceremonies. In this photo Mayor Maguire has just cut the traditional ribbon to open architect Alfred Chapman's masterpiece. The lady in white, an employee of the Health Department, was the pavilion matron.

In engineering terms, the magnificent new bathing pavilion, erected at a cost of $300,000, sprawled a total of 400 feet along the new boulevard traffic way with an overall depth back towards the lake of 120 feet. It had changeroom accommodations for 7,700 bathers with lockers for each patron and separate sections for men and boys, women and girls. There was also a roof garden where light refreshments could be served to 400 guests. The adjacent bathing beach was 1,100 feet in length. Admission fees to the pavilion amounted to 25 cents for adults and 15 cents for children; bathing suits could be rented for 15 cents and towels for 10 cents. There was a special suit and towel combination price of 15 cents for children.

Visitors who drove to Sunnyside could leave their cars in the newly paved parking lots east of the new traffic bridge leading to the King / Queen / Roncesvalles / Lakeshore intersection and south of the Grand Trunk railway tracks.

For those who came to the new park somewhat short of money, the City operated what was called a "free bathing beach" just east of the mouth of the Humber River. Access to this beach was one of the reasons why the city streetcars were extended to a new loop at the Humber.

Above

Built in 1917, five years before the Sunnyside Bathing Pavilion and Amusement park opened, the structure shown here was known as the Sunnyside Pavilion Restaurant and served the public during the waterfront redevelopment program. The restaurant was located on the south side of the old Lake Shore Road, right on the site of the once-popular restaurant operated by Mrs. Pauline Myers, and backed onto Lake Ontario. The *Star Weekly* of August 13, 1921, described the establishment in terms perhaps better understood sixty years ago:

> The pavilion itself is Italian architecture, built in wings, with two spacious gardens joined by a covered walk. In one wing all kinds of ices and sandwiches and iced drinks are served á la carte. In the other, where a wonderful polished dancing floor is sunk, there is a minimum charge of $1.50 per couple, 75¢ per person, and that includes dancing privileges on the outside floor. Also included in this price is the privilege of ordering up to 75¢ worth of refreshments per person.
>
> Inside the charge is $3 per person, $1.50 single, with amusement tax extra. This figure includes a table d'hôte dinner or ordering à la carte to that amount. The dining-room, where they also dance, is very artistically lighted with cool mauve silk shades throwing such a pretty soft light on the dancers. Here there is a big, comfortable open fireplace where, on a cool night, a fire could be lit and lend another attractive glow to the softly lighted room.
>
> One garden has a profusion of pink and red geranium boxes and it resembles a Venetian garden divided off in terraces and sections, truly Italian. Here also is a fountain coming out of the wall like the gardens in Italy. Over all are two huge reflecting electric lights that illuminate the garden to the farthest corner.
>
> The orchestra here is really brilliant and makes the popular pieces almost classics by introducing so many really clever little "tit-bits." They render for you one of the popular strains with so many airs and graces and novelties added that you hardly recognize the popular air you once knew by the *chef d'oeuvre* that they entertain you with.

Interior of the Sunnyside Pavilion Restaurant, *circa* 1920.

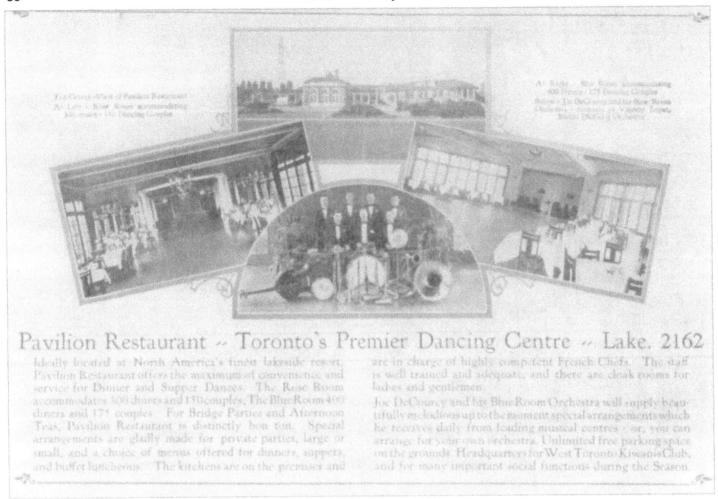

Pavilion Restaurant -- Toronto's Premier Dancing Centre -- Lake. 2162

Sunnyside Pavilion Restaurant brochure, *circa* 1925.

Opposite

By 1920, the popularity of the Pavilion Restaurant had become so great that the original 1917 structure had to be enlarged, effectively doubling its size. However, as a result of the massive land-filling operations that had taken place south of the restaurant, that created both a new Humber Bay and shoreline, what had been the back of the restaurant suddenly became the building's new front facing onto a newly created Lakeshore Boulevard. As a result the building had to be completely redesigned and the top photo shows how it appeared in 1924. For the next dozen years the Pavilion Restaurant was regarded as one of the city's finest dining spots. It had two large dining areas, the Rose Room and the Blue Room, separated by a central kitchen. In the summer months, a large open-air garden provided an additional dining area. In 1936, a new feature on the Toronto scene appeared when William Beasley renovated the restaurant and presented to the public the Club Esquire, complete with the Rhumba Room that would quickly become one the country's best-known evening entertainment venues. One of Beasley's long-time employees remembers the Club Esquire as one of the finest supper clubs on the continent, featuring fine meals, exciting entertainment, and huge painted wall murals depicting faraway beaches lined with white palm trees.

Stage shows, produced by a New York impresario, featuring eight showgirls, eight chorus girls, and supper dancing to the music of Trump Davidson, Ozzie Williams, or Jimmy Namaro, made it the most electrifying place on the Toronto night-life scene. But, there was never any liquor served – not legally, that is.

In 1941, Beasley turned his efforts to other things and once again the place was remodelled and a new name affixed to the front of the building. A company called Parklyn Holdings created a new, and in many eyes, less elegant club known as the Club Top Hat. Over the years the Top Hat, minus the murals and palm trees, featured the orchestras of Cy McLean (the first all black band in Canada), Gordon Delamont, and Frank Bogart. When site grading for the new waterfront expressway commenced in the mid-1950s, the Club Top Hat's days were numbered, and in 1956 the multi-faceted structure was demolished.

Evolution
of a
building

1924

1936

1941

Parkdale Canoe Club, July 1911.

Part of the Sunnyside scene for three-quarters of a century, the Parkdale Canoe Club was organized in 1906 with
twenty enthusiasts meeting for the first few years in a
shack adjacent to the Humber River and then in the basement of Mrs. Meyer's popular lakefront restaurant. Then,
in 1908 the members opened their first real clubhouse in
a small wooden structure erected along the old shoreline
near the foot of Indian Road. This building was destroyed
by fire in 1912 and almost immediately a new clubhouse
was built, but this time, with the Harbour Commission's
new waterfront design in mind, the new structure was
erected much further south and accessed via a long, wood-
en pier. This new facility also caught fire before it was
completed and it wasn't until 1915 that the new home
was finally ready. As the photographs on pages 59 and 60
show, this third clubhouse was a handsome building with
an attractive tile roof and rambling balconies on two sides
from which spectators could watch the numerous regat-
tas and races sponsored by the club.

On April 28, 1923, this clubhouse, by now right on the
water's edge as a result of the landfilling portion of the
massive waterfront development program, also succumbed to flames. Once again, the membership ordered
the construction of a new facility and within a year the
present structure was completed. The name Parkdale
Canoe Club was eventually changed to the Boulevard
Club, and while over the years many changes and addi-
tions have been made to the 1924 building, the letters
PCC on the club's burgee can still be seen over the win-
dows on the north wall, adjacent to the entrance walkway.

Parkdale Canoe Club, July 1920.

Of particular interest are the steel towers that appear in this and the preceding photograph. They were erected by the Hydro Electric Power Commission of Ontario (now Ontario Hydro) during the period 1910–11 to carry the power lines connecting the hydro-electric plants at Niagara Falls with the distribution system in the City of Toronto. Actually, the city's first supply of electricity had come from local coal-fired plants. The arrival on May 2, 1911, of electricity produced at Niagara Falls and transmitted to Toronto over 110,000-volt power lines marked the first time that electricity generated by water power had been put to use in the city.

By observing the location of the towers in these photos, and comparing that location with views of the same towers later in the book, the reader can appreciate how extensive the land reclamation program was in the Sunnyside area. The high-tension lines have since been buried.

Watching the Regatta, Parkdale Canoe Club, April 27,
1923, the day before the fire.

SUNNYSIDE BEACH

The Ideal Place to Enjoy Yourself on

Civic Holiday

MONDAY, AUGUST 3RD

BAND CONCERT--Afternoon and Evening

LADIES' EXHIBITION SOFTBALL GAMES

Afternoon—*London vs. Supremes*
Evening—*London vs. Karrys*

—Also—

WHIPPET RACES

Swimming Races and Diving Contests in
CANADA'S LARGEST POOL
During Afternoon

Every Day a Swimming Day at Sunnyside

GRAY LINE MOTOR COACH SERVICE
(Via Lakeshore Boulevard Drive)

ROUND TRIP 50c (Stop-over at Sunnyside)

First Coach Leaves Front and Yonge Streets 6.30 p.m.
All Coaches Call at Downtown Hotels
Last Coach Leaves Sunnyside Beach 11 p.m.

Parkdale Canoe Club, May 19, 1925.

Just to the east of the club in this photograph is the Sunnyside Stadium where talented competitors in three women's leagues, the Major, Sunnyside and National, played softball in front of huge crowds from the day the diamond opened, May 19, 1925, until the field was bulldozed in 1956 to allow the Boulevard Club to erect ... a parking lot.

Come to the

SUNNYSIDE STADIUM

Tomorrow – Tuesday – June 10th

Two Great Softball Games:

7:00 p.m.—
CROFTONS vs. BRAMPTON

8:30 p.m.—
SUNDAY MORNING CLASS vs. PARAMOUNTS

Between Games—"A" Corps Signals and 2nd Divisional Signals, Royal Canadian Corps of Signals (CA) (R), headed by their brass bands, will parade into the Stadium and be inspected by Colonel E. Forde, D.S.O., V.D., Officer Administering Royal Canadian Corps Signals in Canada.

LUCKY DRAW — ACTION MUSIC

All Proceeds to the Women's Auxiliary, R.C.C.S., for Comforts for the Fighting Signals.

DON'T MISS IT TOMORROW NIGHT!

This Advertisement is donated to the R.C.C.S. Auxiliary by CKCL

Built at a cost of $80,000, what we now know as the Palais Royale originally housed Walter Dean's boat-building factory. Until moving to the Sunnyside area, Dean had been in the pleasure craft building business for years, first in a ramshackled old shack near the foot of York Street, then in a small building near the Grand Trunk steam railway crossing at the foot of today's Roncesvalles Avenue. When work began on the new amusement park, Dean negotiated with the Harbour Commission for a new building and one was built for him at a cost of $80,000. It was in this new structure that Dean was to become famous for his eagerly sought-after "Sunnyside Torpedo Canoe."

For a time, and as a special promotion while the park was being created, anyone over sixteen years of age visiting Dean's new Sunnyside factory and purchasing one of the "Torpedos" was given two free hours of paddling (except on Wednesday or Saturday) in the lake directly south of the boat-house and factory.

On June 28, 1922, the same day that the park opened, the new Palais Royale dance hall moved into the upper level of the factory and boat-building operations were relocated to the basement. Not long after, Walter Dean retired and moved north to Coldwater, Ontario. Under the management of Bill Cuthbert and George Deller, the Palais Royale quickly became the most popular dance hall in the entire city. Over the years virtually every Canadian and American "big band" appeared at the Palais Royale, including Toronto's own Bert Niosi, who was to lead the Palais' house band for many years. Big band dances are still held at the Palais Royale and people come from miles around to "swing and sway" and dance the night away.

The late radio and TV personality Elwood Glover remembers Sunnyside and the Palais Royale this way:

For me, Sunnyside began in 1938. A green kid from the West had come to the big city to seek fame and fortune and was in awe of everything a big city represented – theatres, museums, art galleries, and dance bands! Entertainment was my fascination in those days, and I remember being taken to Sunnyside on my first Sunday evening

in Toronto where the lights and crowds and noise recreated for me all the excitement of a country fair except that Sunnyside had a real live thundering roller-coaster and a super luxurious merry-go-round. No matter where you went the enchanting fragrance of hot dogs, mustard, and fried onions followed your every step.

I remember Cuthbert and Deller's Palais Royale, where Bert Niosi's band played nightly, was just a few hundred yards to the east. It was a veritable magnet that drew me to every visiting name band that played there with one appearing on stage at least every two weeks in the late thirties; Count Basie, Duke Ellington, Jack Teagarden, Bob Crosby, and Glen Gray. Imagine, in August of 1938, four straight nights of Artie Shaw and his band, during which he plugged a new record he'd just cut and was trying hard to turn into a hit. The song? "Begin the Beguine."

I also remember a bandshell with its back to the lake where every Sunday night a People's Credit Jewellers radio broadcast would take place. It had a dynamic M.C. named Stan Francis who would hold a thousand people in the palm of his hand and have them singing like crazy.

Sunnyside was a summer wonderland that I'm surprised Toronto can get along without. I can still smell the fried onions!

Walter Dean

These photos were taken in 1914 and look west *(top)* and east along the waterfront at Sunnyside. As previously described the steel towers were erected by the Hydro Electric Power Commission of Ontario to carry the 110,000-volt high tension power lines from Niagara Falls to Toronto. In the background of the top view we can see the recently constructed traffic bridge that led from the busy Queen / King / Roncesvalles intersection down to the old Lakeshore Road. To the extreme right is the Sunnyside railway station that stood, until the early 1960s, on the south side of King Street at the foot of Roncesvalles Avenue. Over the years land-filling operations resulted in the shoreline being pushed many hundreds of feet to the south and, as the photos on pages 68 and 69 reveal, the new Lakeshore Boulevard was constructed almost in line with these towers.

In 1921, under the direction of the Harbour Commission's E.L. Cousins, work began on an extremely ambitious program that was given the title "The Marginal Boulevard" and was described as a thoroughfare that would become "one of the greatest scenic traffic ways in any city in Eastern Canada." The boulevard was to make a complete loop around the city (as defined by the Humber, Lawrence Avenue, and the Don Valley to Victoria Park Avenue) and extend along the waterfront with an alternate route over the east and west gaps and across the Island.

The top photo shows clearing operations underway just east of the old Humber Bay. Sooty, black smoke, from one of the steam dredges used to pump thousands of cubic yards of muck from the bottom of the bay that would then be piped to shore through a floating pipeline to create a new shoreline, smudges the skyline. The muck would be dressed with top soil brought in from the Commission's farm in Pickering.

Towers erected by the Hydro Electric Power Commission of Ontario, now Ontario Hydro, are situated well inland in this 1919 photograph. When originally constructed their massive concrete footings were deep in the waters of the old Humber Bay. Land reclamation has pushed the shoreline several hundred feet south and we can see the Marginal Boulevard beginning to take shape. This photograph was taken from the old Wilson Avenue footbridge and shows the extent of boulevard construction in late 1919. To the right are the tracks of the Grand Trunk Railway (which became part of CNR in 1923 and are now used extensively by GO and VIA passenger trains), and in the background the railway station and the new Lakeshore Bridge at the foot of Roncesvalles Avenue.

Work on the new Marginal Boulevard Driveway began in 1919 and by the end of 1920 the fifty-four-foot-wide thoroughfare, now known as Lakeshore Boulevard West, was opened as far east as Wilson (now Wilson Park) Avenue. On December 22 of the next year the extension to Dowling Avenue was ready for traffic and officially opened by Mayor Tommy Church. By August 26, 1922, the boulevard, now three miles in length, was completed as far as the west entrance to the CNE.

Coincident with the construction of the Marginal Boule-vard Driveway work proceeded on building a magnificent wooden boardwalk of white pine from the Humber River to Wilson (now Wilson Park) Avenue. The boardwalk, described by the newspapers as "Toronto's Atlantic City boardwalk," was to be twenty-four-feet wide with the section from Wilson Avenue to Dowling Avenue sixteen feet in width. From that point to the west entrance of Exhibition Park it was to be simply poured concrete. In this 1920 photograph we see work underway just south of the Pavilion Restaurant which can be seen to the right of centre under one of the new hydro towers.

David Crombie, former Mayor of Toronto, grew up in nearby Swansea. He remembers Sunnyside with these words:

> Sunnyside was a world just outside our neighbour-hood. From our house you walked to the bottom of the street passing Catfish Pond and the Camels' Hump hills on the right and the mysteries of Grenadier Pond and the promises of High Park on the left. Just as you came out from under the rail-

> way bridge, by the old Lake Simcoe ice-house, you could feel the charge as the village met the lake.

> Across the short field and a narrow Lakeshore Road we would run to get to our first goal – the boardwalk! That boardwalk was a great pathway to imagined pleasures. A kind of yellow-brick road that stretched as far as the eye could see and where you could feel the excitement as the boards warmed your feet in the summer sun.

> And there it was! The water, the breakwall, the colours, the people, the smells, the happy noise – the sheer energy of it all. A world of rides, Honey Dew, music, and chips with vinegar and salt.

Both the new Sunnyside Bathing Pavilion and the Pavilion Restaurant (later the Club Esquire and, later still, the Top Hat) are evident in this 1922 photo that looks west along the still incomplete Lakeshore Boulevard that would convey vehicular traffic from the Humber River to Queen and King streets, via the steel traffic bridge that was erected in 1912 over the busy mainline railway tracks.

Toronto Transportation (after 1954 Transit) Commission crews are shown erecting the overhead for a streetcar right of way that, over the years, would have five different TTC routes operating over it:

King (from July 26, 1922, until July 1, 1923).

Beach (from July 1, 1923, until December 9, 1928).

Mimico (January 12, 1927, until December 9, 1928).

Lakeshore (from December 9, 1928, until August 2, 1937).

Queen (from August 3, 1937, until July 21, 1957, when the *Queen* streetcars were rerouted to operate along a private right of way in the centre of the newly constructed Queensway that had opened to vehicular traffic on December 10, 1956).

In this progress photo the extent of boulevard and boardwalk construction up to April 1922 can be seen. The house
to the right would soon be demolished to permit work to
start on the new parking lots for people driving to the
amusement park. In the centre background the cupola of
the old Ocean House Hotel at the southeast corner of the
King, Queen, and Roncesvalles intersection can be seen.
This building, minus its cupola, still stands. Also visible
in the background to the left are the bridge over the railway tracks, the Sunnyside station, and, behind the towers, St. Joseph's Hospital. In the centre background are
the buildings along King Street, many of which are still
there.

Fire destroyed the Parkdale Canoe Club again on April 28, 1923, and the ruins of the building can be seen in this photo taken several days later. The heavy auto traffic on the Boulevard Driveway (now Lakeshore Boulevard West), some hearty souls on the new boardwalk, and a portion of the parking lots described on the previous page are also evident. The hydro towers still straddle the boulevard. Another two years (and a few car accidents) would pass before they were moved out of the way. The Sunnyside merry-go-round and Flyer roller-coaster loom in the background and, to the extreme right, overlooking the park, is a portion of the hospital.

As is evident in the lower photo, it wasn't long after the new Boulevard Driveway opened that the area experienced its first traffic jam.

In the **above** photo workmen complete the landscaping around the new bandstand that had been erected in 1922 across the partially completed boulevard from Deans' boat factory. Several years later it became necessary, because of the thunderous band organ music emanating from the newly constructed Derby Racer, to move the stand to a new location at the end of a short pier jutting out into the lake. The bandstand in its new location can be seen in the top photograph on the next page.

In early 1929, extremely high water levels did severe damage to the bathing beaches, resulting in another massive reclamation project. More than 225,000 cubic feet of sand were dredged from the lake and deposited on the shore between the bathing pavilion and Parkdale Canoe Club. Again, the bandstand was surrounded by a dry sandy beach as seen in the top photograph on page 73.

Advertised as having "the dippiest dips on the continent"
the Sunnyside Flyer, which was designed by A.J. Miller,
a veteran amusement ride builder who built most of the
attractions at Hanlan's Point, was erected in 1923. Miller
had designed almost ninety percent of the roller-coasters
on the North American continent, as well as four huge
structures at Blackpool, England. In a *Mail & Empire*
newspaper interview, Miller described a roller-coaster as
a direct descendant of the old "switchback railway" that
carried coal out of the Allegheny Mountains and stated
that the first such amusement ride operated in Philadelphia in 1888. "Roller-coasters were built so young men
and women could meet each other and for parents who
want to be good sports to their children," Miller went on.
In 1933, Miller redesigned the Flyer and it was said that
on this "new" coaster, cars would reach sixty miles per
hour when "coming home."

Roller-coasters continue to be extremely popular
attractions at the world's innumerable amusement parks.
At Canada's Wonderland, the nation's first theme park
that opened in 1981 just north of Toronto, there are three
wooden roller-coasters, the Ghoaster Coaster, the Wilde
Beast, and the Mighty Canadian Minebuster.

Another tradition at Sunnyside Amusement Park, complimenting the rides, games and hot dogs, was a cooling drink called Honey Dew. Developed by the Ryan brothers in 1916, Honey Dew was first marketed at the old Pavlova Roller Rink on Cowan Avenue, just south of Queen Street West. This old structure, which was also known as Masaryk Hall, still stands.

Honey Dew Limited was incorporated in 1928 and at that time operated five restaurants and two concession booths in the city, one of which was this structure under renovation at Sunnyside in 1936. In 1943, Honey Dew Limited became part of Canadian Food Products Limited.

Another popular beverage available at Sunnyside was Hires Root Beer. This drink has an interesting history going back to the year 1869 when a young Philadelphia pharmacist, Charles E. Hires, concocted an extract of various roots, herbs, and barks which he sold in powder form in small packages. The customer would steep the powder in boiling water, drain, cool, and serve. As the years went by the product's popularity grew to such an extent that more convenient packaging was needed. Soon a three-ounce bottle hit the shelves all across the States. Now the customer only had to add sugar, yeast, and water to make a delicious instant carbonated drink. In fact, Hires Root Beer was the first soft drink to become a national favourite. In Toronto, Hires Root Beer was blended in a small plant on Davies Avenue and was available at the park right from the opening day. Hires remained a family-run business until 1960 when the company was sold to Consolidated Foods Corporation. Two years later Hires became part of Crush International.

Another favourite drink was Vernor's ginger ale. Bottled by the old Bernard Beverage Company on Bathurst Street just north of King, Vernor's was, like several other popular soft drinks, developed by a pharmacist.

In 1861, young James Vernor of Detroit, Michigan, went to war, but before leaving mixed several secret ingredients together and stored the concoction in a large wooden keg. Four years later the Civil War ended and Vernor, the returned veteran, opened a drug store on Woodward Avenue in his home city. To be a *real* drug store it had to have a soda fountain with a special and exclusive beverage "on fount," as they said in those days. Vernor had his – the mixture he had left to age before going off to war. The drink's popularity grew slowly in the immediate area at first, but by 1915 Vernor's Ginger Ale had become popular enough to necessitate the construction of a special bottling plant. The market continued to grow and in the 1930s Vernor's made its appearance in Toronto. The drink, with its little gnome logo, became an instant hit at Sunnyside.

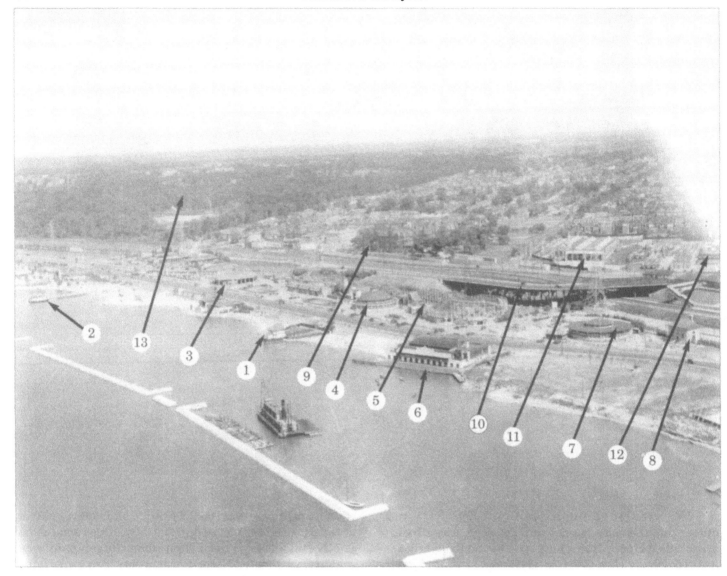

This aerial view of Sunnyside was taken in 1926 shortly after the Merrymakers Stage (shown on the water's edge just above the dredge moored near the breakwall, #1) was built. It was on this stage that Captain Merton Plunkett, founder of the popular First World War vaudeville group called the Dumbells, performed with many of his wartime buddies as well as acts such as the Singing Watson Sisters, James and Arthur Yule, comedians *extraordinaire*, and others. The Merrymakers Stage lasted until the mid 1930s. So well known was this attraction that an American producer had sought, unsuccessfully, to broadcast the immensely popular Major Bowes' Amateur Hour radio show from the Merrymakers Stage.

Some of the other prominent buildings in this view are: #2, the bandstand, where the T.T.C.'s Toronto Concert Band frequently played; #3, Pavilion Restaurant (later Club Esquire, later still, Club Top Hat); #4, merry-go-round; #5, Flyer roller-coaster; #6, Palais Royale and Deans' boathouse; #7, Derby Racer; and #8, a municipal pumping station that still stands on the north side of Lakeshore Boulevard.

North of the amusement park we can see: #9, St. Joseph's Hospital and the old Sunnyside Villa; #10, Sunnyside traffic bridge; #11, the T.T.C.'s Roncesvalles carhouse; #12, the Sunnyside railway station; and #13, High Park.

The artist's sketch above depicts a proposal put forward by the Harbour Commission's Chief Engineer E.L. Cousins, who recommended that an exclusive apartment complex similar to Chicago's Lincoln Park be developed across the new boulevard from the new $300,000 bathing pavilion. This imaginative idea never got off the drawing board.

The Toronto Harbour Commission's 1912 idea for a recreation area along the water's edge for the pleasure of the citizens of Toronto certainly wasn't the first time this type of plan had been put forward. Exactly sixty years earlier John George Howard, the City Surveyor of the day who resided in Colborne Lodge, High Park, drew up the plan shown below. His plan featured pleasure and carriage drives, walks, and shrubbery landscaping between the shoreline of Toronto Bay and Front Street. No doubt Howard would be pleased to learn that modern pleasure places such as a proposed golf course (to be developed east of Bathurst Street), a proposed museum (in the former CPR roundhouse), and a newly created park (to be called Roundhouse Park) now all sit on the site of his pleasure grounds. The sprawling Metro Toronto Convention Centre and new addition also sit astride Howard's 1852 pleasure ground concept.

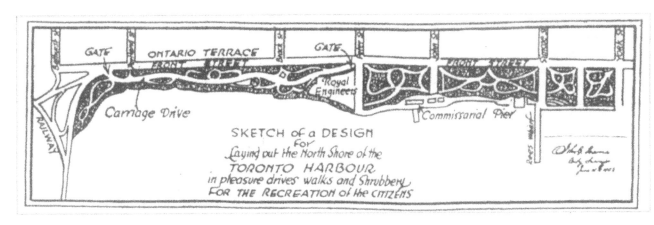

Perhaps in an effort to justify the tremendous cost of building the new swimming facility at the park, the bathing pavilion was officially called the Sunnyside Outdoor Natatorium, though most people simply called it the Sunnyside tank (never pool, thank you, and if you did call it the pool, you obviously weren't from the Sunnyside area). This $75,000 structure was opened on July 29, 1925, by Tommy Church seen on the megaphone in the above photograph doing the honours. Tommy had served as mayor of Toronto from 1915 to 1921 and then as a member of the provincial parliament, a position he held for a full quarter of a century.

Built in just seventy-eight days three years after the nearby bathing pavilion first opened, the tank had become an absolute necessity following two unseasonably cold summer seasons that had resulted in very few bathers using either the pavilion's change rooms or the beach area.

The new Sunnyside tank was of huge proportions, 300 feet by 75 feet, and could accommodate 2,000 swimmers. At one time it was recognized as the largest outdoor pool in the world. Admission fees were set at 35¢ for adults and 10¢ for children, with $6 and $2 season passes also available (if you could afford them). Today, there are no admission fees to the tank which has been renamed the Gus Ryder – Sunnyside Pool, although to true Sunnysiders it's still just "the tank."

Sam "The Record Man" Sniderman has these memories of Sunnyside and its bathing tank:

To many Torontonians, including myself, in the 1920s the Sunnyside area, nestled along the lake front between the Humber River on the west and Exhibition Park on the east, was the focal point of our courting and social activities from April to September. And, with the Toronto Islands somewhat out of bounds to many of us, Sunnyside was our only chance for a holiday resort and a respite from the city's hot months of July and August. As we waited in line with sweaty dimes clutched in our hands for admittance to the always crowded tank area, we welcomed the chance to parade like peacocks showing off our suntanned muscles.

At the west end of this midway-like complex were the drive-it-yourself miniature autos. An anxiously looked forward to two-minute-ride around the track was a once-a-week delight for this six-year-old. Sometimes, on very special occasions, like on your birthday, you'd go around a second time. Moving east, teenagers hustled their dates on the rides and in turn were hustled themselves at the gaming stands as they competed against stupendous odds displaying their prowess, trying to win their girls a treasured souvenir.

Grandmothers with grandchildren in prams, soldiers on
leave, families on an outing, and just ordinary pals loved
Sunnyside.

Four
The Golden Years

Toronto's Sunnyside Amusement Park, which was built by the Toronto Harbour Commission and basked in the sun on the shore of Humber Bay, was a success from the very day it opened, June 28, 1922. So much so that within a few years its original seven rides, nine games, and ten food concessions had grown to eight rides, fourteen games, and nineteen food outlets. And while the increase in the number of rides doesn't seem large it was significant that many of the smaller rides, like the low-level swings, were replaced by much more costly and sophisticated rides such as the Flyer roller-coaster in 1923 and Derby Racer in 1924.

Starting in 1923 the Dutch Mill entertained thousands of visitors, and three years later the ever-popular House of Fun was introduced. A golf-putting course appeared in 1923, as did games such as Park Your Car and Pick Your Colour. In 1924, the Victor Talking Machine company's Auditorium Orthophonic Victrola was presented to astonished Sunnyside audiences. This attraction was, in reality, a giant Victrola complete with a series of vacuum tubes that was capable of playing records at volumes never before accomplished. It was reported that Sousa could be heard up on Queen Street!

In 1925, what was to become a huge crowd pleaser, ladies' softball, was introduced to Sunnyside's patrons. On the other hand newspaper accounts reveal, in no uncertain terms, that the introduction of pay toilets in 1925 was definitely not a popular move. That measure was rescinded the following year. As popular as the rides, games, and food stands were, they certainly weren't the only drawing cards. Sunnyside employed some very clever showmen who devised various unique, exciting, and sometimes downright silly attractions in an attempt to entice larger and larger crowds to the park. Let's look at some of those attractions.

In 1923 there was a huge corn roast and Tiny Tim, the dancing bear, made an appearance. A few years later, someone called Harry Lehman, an escape artist, was buried alive. (Incidentally, he did escape.) In 1927 there was a female impersonators competition (Is there nothing new?), a series of Ukrainian song and dance performances, and daylight fireworks spectacles. The next year marathon swimmer George Young, "the Catalina Kid," made an appearance at the tank, a freckled-faced, red-haired kid contest was held, sea fleas appeared at the lakefront, and 641 mothers entered their babies in a contest that must have been a real howl especially when you consider that there had to be 640 losers. In 1929, Prince Notaes Masahara, the world famous mind reader, visited

the park, as did Pickard's Performing Seals and the *Ballet Canadienne*. So, too, did airplane wing-walker Bobby Irwin, who several years earlier had replaced an act at Sunnyside that featured Miss Carolyn Sykes, a young girl who, while performing a parachute demonstration, almost drowned in Humber Bay. The year 1929 saw the start of what in retrospect was a rather lamentable series of events, the burning of old ships moored to the Sunnyside breakwall. Forty-five-year-old *John Hanlan* was the first to go, followed by four others over the next few years, including *Lyman Davis*, the last wooden schooner on the Great Lakes. These historic blazing hulks were great for attracting crowds.

The year 1930 almost saw the introduction of sight-seeing flights over the city when the idea was put forward by Interlake Airways. A Fokker seaplane was to be used, but the proposal was rejected when the company insisted on using the area inside the breakwall as the landing strip.

The season wasn't a total loss, however. Park authorities did give away two ponies (I can see Dad's face now) and held several honest-to-goodness Calithumpian parades. Then on June 20 George Bennet attempted a parachute jump. His equipment malfunctioned and he fell onto the Lakeshore Boulevard breaking his back. For weeks Bennet hovered near death while the city prayed. Several fundraising events were held at the park and, happily, the lucky daredevil eventually recovered.

The following year something else fell out of an airplane, but this time it was just a Masterbilt watch. Unfortunately, records concerning this rather strange promotion don't reveal what happened to either the watch or to the heads of the visitors at the park. The *Star* newspaper sponsored a comic strip dress-up parade that was to be followed the next week by the appearance of a pack of performing pigs. Unfortunately, this last event was put on the back burner (not literally, I hope) before it even got started.

There was an interesting proposal put forward in 1931 when a consultant suggested the restaurant be turned into an aquarium full of creatures found in the Great Lakes. They served fish dinners instead. As the Great Depression deepened it became harder and harder to attract cash-strapped visitors. As a result, 1933 was an extremely busy one for the park's attractions manager. In addition to many events that had been tried in years past, there was a surf-boarding demonstration (surf in Humber Bay?), followed by the popular "Harry Hornes' Radio Hour" that was broadcast coast-to-coast from the park. "Shipwreck" Kelly, the world-renowned flag-pole sitter, made a return appearance and drew thousands to the park to watch him sit ... on a flag-pole. In addition, many of the rides received extensive renovations. The next year, 1934, a dishwashing contest was held, the Hopi cliff-dwellers made an appearance, and special events were held honouring the city's centennial. In 1936, amateur wrestling bouts were presented on the Merrymakers Stage, and for two weeks in July the park was converted into a huge outside bedroom as thousands slept along the Sunnyside shoreline seeking relief from a week-long searing heatwave that included two days, July 9 and 10, when the mercury soared to a record shattering 40.5 degrees Centigrade.

In 1938, Mary Pickford attended a softball game and created incredible traffic problems, and in 1939 another attraction, the Sabras Dance Pavilion, drew thousands to the park. Following the outbreak of war many flag-waving recruiting attractions were held at the park, including frequent artillery demonstrations using the howitzers of the 21st Battalion of the 7th Toronto Regiment. In July of 1945, a contingent of 130 Russian soldiers were welcome visitors to the park, while a year later five unwelcome German prisoners of war from the Cooksville internment camp were recaptured as they tried to sneak into the Palais Royale dance hall. That same year the park held a "handsomest man" contest and two years later, 1948, Captain Tiebor's trained seals barked on cue, balanced rubber balls on their noses, and, all in all, behaved quite properly. But something must have gone wrong with Prince Kigor's lion-taming act, though. Looking at the first newspaper advertisement for his act reveals that he worked with "trained lions." A few days later the ad was changed to read "untamed lions." Mmmmm!

Gas and tire rationing during the Second World War had forced Torontonians to stay close to home, resulting in tremendous crowds visiting the park during those dark years. But with peace came the urge to build some of those "super highways" the Americans had. One of those super highways would be something called the Lakeshore Expressway and it would be built between the park and the railway tracks. The planners said that it's presence would ease the severe traffic congestion caused by the totally inadequate highways that ran through the Sunnyside area. Now, for most modern-thinking Torontonians, the once popular park was just in the way. By the spring of 1956 Sunnyside Amusement Park was no more.

Top right

Long before Sunnyside Amusement Park opened on the city's western waterfront in 1922, fashion-conscious Torontonians had frequently participated in Easter parades along the old wooden boardwalk in front of Maw's Boat House and Pauline Meyer's Banquet and Refreshment Pavilion. Then, coincident with the construction of the new Lakeshore Boulevard in the early 1920s, the Harbour Commission decided to build a new wooden boardwalk along the south side of the thoroughfare, giving Torontonians a very special place to hold the annual Easter Parade. But it wasn't only at Eastertime that Sunnysiders strutted along the white pine boards; they also came by the thousands in good weather and bad.

In 1934, as part of the relief work program instituted by the city during the misery-filled depression years, a work crew was sent to Sunnyside to replace the badly deteriorated boardwalk. This $26,400 project was carried out by a foreman, ten labourers, and eight carpenters. This latter group earned a princely eighty cents an hour.

In the late 1930s, and right through the war years, thousands continued the tradition of Easter, parading the Sunnyside boardwalk even though the wooden walkway continued to deteriorate at an ever-increasing rate.

Bottom right

The last big Easter parade at Sunnyside was held in 1953. The following year Torontonians flocked to fashionable Bloor Street, between Yonge and Bay, to do their parading. Sam "the Record Man" Sniderman gives us this memory of the Sunnyside parade:

> At Easter time we paraded our once-a-year outfits on the boardwalk having converged on Sunnyside via the jam-packed streetcars and traffic-jammed streets that still meet like spokes of a wheel at the heights overlooking that great ghost-of-the-past place. Back and forth 'till fatigue or frustration overtook us and, if 25¢ was affordable, we'd retreat to a nearby food stand for a Honey Dew and hot dog or a Downyflake donut and coffee.

In these three views of the famed Sunnyside boardwalk we see (**top left**) a city works crew during the Great Depression rebuilding a portion of the walk as part of a relief project. Note the stack of badly rotted timbers sitting to the right of the photo. By the late thirties paychecks had started to increase in size, as had the crowds strolling along the boardwalk. The photo at the (**bottom left**) looks east along the boardwalk from in front of the Sunnyside bathing pavilion.

The increased popularity of the boardwalk contributed once again to severe deterioration of the planking, as can be seen in the (**above photograph**) taken soon after the end of the war. Note that some of the visitors are still in uniform. This time, there were no plans to rehabilitate the landmark and it was left to rot and decay until the only recourse was its removal and replacement with asphalt.

The winter had been particularly hard and Torontonians flocked to Sunnyside on Easter Sunday, 1949, to absorb some of the eagerly sought-after early spring sunshine. Obviously it was still too early to fill the Sunnyside "tank" with the required 750,000 gallons of recirculated and filtered water that would be kept at a constant 68 degrees Fahrenheit. This view shows the covered spectator bleachers that used to be located at the east end of the tank, as well as the benches on the north and south sides. The tank is still in operation although the seating has been removed and, unlike the so-called good old days, now there is no admission charge.

The view also shows the serious traffic bottleneck that resulted from the fact that the park's location straddled what was then the main western artery leading into and out of Toronto. Today, eastbound traffic on Lakeshore Boulevard uses the traffic lanes that are occupied by two-way traffic in this photo. To the left of the view is Lakeshore Road leading to the Sunnyside Bridge and the often chaotic Queen / King / Roncesvalles / Lakeshore intersection. In 1957, the bridge was pulled down and Lakeshore Road was extended through the recently cleared amusement park grounds and became part of the new westbound lanes of Lakeshore Boulevard.

Another long-time Sunnyside tradition was the "free bathing car" service. Instituted in the 1890s by the operators of the privately owned Toronto Railway Company and carried on by the Toronto Transportation Commission after its formation in 1921, special "free bathing cars" would roam various routes throughout the city picking up children who carried a bathing suit and towel and transporting them, free, to Sunnyside. Return trips along the same routes would take place later in the day. An *Evening Telegram* cartoonist gives us a quaint look at this service in his contribution to the August 19, 1922 edition of the paper. To give some idea of the extent of the service, here is a list of routes for the free bathing car service to the park during the summer of 1934:

King – Leaving Jane Street loop at 1:10 pm, east along Bloor to Dundas, south on Dundas and Roncesvalles to King, then east along King to unloading point near Wilson Avenue.

Dundas – Leaving Runnymede loop at 1:20 pm, south on Dundas and Roncesvalles to King, then east along King to unloading point.

Dovercourt – Leaving Townsley loop at 1:08 pm, south on Weston Road to Davenport, east along Davenport to Dovercourt, south on Dovercourt to College, east along College to Ossington, south on Ossington to Queen, west along Queen to Sunnyside loop, then return east along King to unloading point.

Lansdowne – Leaving Royce loop at 1:34 pm, south on Lansdowne to Dundas, west along Dundas and Howard Park Avenue to Roncesvalles, south on Roncesvalles to King, east along King to unloading point.

Bathurst – Leaving Keele loop at 1:03 pm, east along St. Clair to Bathurst, south on Bathurst to Queen, west along Queen to Sunnyside loop, return east via King to unloading point.

Carlton – Leaving Danforth carhouse at 12:40 pm, south on Coxwell to Gerrard, west along Gerrard to Parliament, south on Parliament to Queen, west along Queen to Sunnyside loop, then return

east along King to unloading point.

Note: all free bathing cars will display "Private" route signs and special "Bathing Car" destination signs.

Returning cars will leave Sunnyside between 3:30 and 4 o'clock.

In this day of rush, rush, rush, it's difficult to appreciate both the small-town quaintness and extreme popularity of the "free bathing car." In the summer of 1930 Toronto *Mail and Empire* reporter Jessie MacTaggart captured this special mood in an article titled "Policeman Rejoices in the Role of Pied Pier of Sunnyside":

"Uncle Smitty" is a policeman. He is in Cowan Avenue division and his number is 422. But the number of his "nieces and nephews" is myriad.

P.C. Harry Smith is the pied piper of Sunnyside. He has played that role ever since the TTC took over the free swimming cars provided for Toronto's schoolchildren. He has perhaps more juvenile friends than any other man in Toronto.

Tall, lean, bronzed yesterday afternoon he lead his army of happy yelling youngsters up the steps to King Street from the beach at Sunnyside. He turned to wave his willow wand at a straggler. "Get back there in line," he ordered sternly. The straggler jumped back. P.C. Smith gazed ahead and smiled. He was happy. Another year had brought him back to his youngsters.

Yesterday was the second day of this year's season of free swims. Old friendships were being renewed and new acquaintances made. "Hello Uncle, hello Uncle Smitty" came from all sides as the tall policeman, one moment frowning, the next smiling, mischievously arranged his little people in rows on King Street to board the special street cars. Citizens came out on their verandahs to watch and motorists stopped to gaze with interest.

"*Bathurst* here," he waved his wand to a section chalked off on the curb. "*Dovercourt* there," and so on, 'till the army was strung along the roadside in groups. The TTC inspector, pad in hand, counted heads. "Hey there, who shouldn't be here?

Only seven came on a *King*, and now there's nine." Two boys called out, "We came on a *Queen* but are going home on a *King*. It's less crowded."

"Alright, as long as you let me know."

Waiting for the street cars to call for their passengers, Uncle Smitty relaxed for a moment to chat.

"Yes, I like the kids," he said. "There's not many here today. It's still a little too cold. But on a warm day, Whew! When we get 2,300 here they sure are a handful." He smiled. Suddenly the smile vanished as he swung around and thundered, "What's going on here?"

An agitated rear rank immediately stilled. "No scrapping, you understand," he ordered as he fixed an unsmiling eye on two small miscreants. "No, I don't have much trouble," he said. Another broad smile. "Most of us are old friends and understand each other. I have to be stern, you know, or I wouldn't be able to do anything with them. You should have seen them the first year. They scrambled around like wild things, trampled those flower beds" – pointing along the curb – "to bits. But the older members understand now and tell the new ones. Why there's a couple of kids been coming ever since they weren't big enough to do up their own pants. They used to yell, "'Come here, Uncle, and do me up!'"

Uncle Smitty walked along, chatting, "Here they are," he said, as a small boy seated on the curb in a front rank plucked at the red-striped trouser leg. "Hello, Uncle, give me your gat," the small boy grinned. "How are you Joey. Where's your brother George, working today?" Uncle Smitty smiled down.

"Yeh, George's working. Give me your gat," the freckled face crewed impudently. The blue-coated arm of the law reached down and chucked little Joey in his overalled stomach. Joey, gurgling with pleasure, rolled over on the grass, as the group applauded.

Joey, it turned out, belongs to a family of six, five members of which are regular "customers." "The mother brought the sixth one down last Summer," Uncle Smitty remarked. "It was just a baby, but I expect it will be here too, one of these days."

"Hey, Uncle, look at my toe," a youngster in the next group called as he wriggled a bare toe through a hole in his running shoe. That started a competition. At least 15 holeful running shoes were displayed by the various candidates and a champion with eight holes was discovered. Uncle

Smitty acted as judge. He ruled out one young man who displayed canvas shoes as yet unsoiled. "Too new," he shook his head.

"Oh, Uncle, you've got lots of holes," cried another as she pointed to the eyelets on the policeman's shining black boot.

"Yeh, but I've got 14 then," replied the young man with the new canvas shoes. Someone began counting the eyelets on Uncle Smitty's shoes. A tiny blonde girl interrupted, "Please, Uncle, he's putting grass down my neck."

Uncle glanced at the offender. "He won't do it again, will you son?" "Son" exchanged an understanding smile, "No, sir," he said.

Just then a street car hove around the corner. "Wheee – " all groups clamoured. "It's ours. It's ours," a group yelled, dancing.

Uncle Smitty, suddenly businesslike, marshalled the youngsters on the car. A little freckled girl hung back to give him a parting smile.

The policeman watched the car depart. "They're dandy kids," he said. "You know, it's funny how pretty some of these youngsters grow up. I've been looking after them for years. Sometimes in the winter a pretty flapper comes along the street, all fixed up fine, and says, "Hello Uncle." Then I knew she's been one of my Sunnyside kids.

"Good-bye. So-long 'till to-morrow." Uncle Smitty waved his hand.

As the popularity of the park began to die, so did the popularity of the free bathing car. The last two such cars ran on August 9, 1950, their complement consisting of a grand total of eight children. The free bathing car service terminated that afternoon.

These two photographs were taken in 1924, just two years after the amusement park opened. For most visitors to Sunnyside their first and last memory was the long staircase leading from the Queen / King / Roncesvalles / Lakeshore intersection down to the park. These steps are still in the writer's memory and while the top photo proves there were not all that many, I'll always remember that staircase as being a mile high.

It was in 1924 that Sunnyside introduced dog racing on the lawn across from the bathing pavilion. History is vague on the particulars on this short-lived attraction at the park, especially as to whether a mechanical or live target was used. What is interesting, however, is the hue and cry that went up fifty years later when the Canadian National Exhibition announced that it was looking into the possibility of holding greyhound racing at the Grandstand. It never happened.

When Sunnyside opened in 1922 there was, in addition to several of the so-called "thrill" rides, one large merry-go-round located at the extreme east end of the amusement park. It's quite possible that this ride came to the park from its original location at Hanlan's Point. Two years later a new merry-go-round called the Derby Racer was built and put into operation just in time for the park's third season. This wasn't just another carousel, however. the Globe newspaper of March 31, 1924, described the new ride, then under construction just to the east of the original merry-go-round, with these words:

Some genius has evolved a new mechanical wonder with which to satisfy the recreative appetite of summer visitors to the Sunnyside amusement area. Its construction has been going on for some weeks. Now it is almost complete. So far as its mechanical components are concerned, it is complete and has just been operated to the complete satisfaction of its supervisors. A ticket booth and a few days of fine weather alone remain to complete it.

The new public toy is simply a group of life-size, mechanical racehorses which conduct a perfectly 'square' race, the outcome of which is unknown even to the operator. A circular track, much after the style of the staid old merry-go-round, constitutes the course. A series of complicated cables, pulleys, runners, and cams control the movements of the horses, but in a manner which defies a non-technical description. Whatever may be the process of operation, this is what happens:

Four would-be jockeys, having purchased their tickets, mount the four life-like steeds. The operator pulls a lever and at a regular pace the horses begin 'trotting' round the course. At a signal another lever is pulled. Then the race starts. No. 1 horse, prancing somewhat in the way a real horse should, might forge slightly ahead. Or perhaps No. 3 or No. 2 or even No. 4 will momentarily attain the lead. This goes on for several minutes. When the race finally ends one horse has won, but which one can be known to no one until then. The unseen mechanism, working purely automatically, alone determines the winner.

That is the new thriller which Mr. "Lol" Solman and his amusement company have thought out for the edification of summer pleasure-seekers. It may receive its introduction about May 1. If the weatherman is kind the first week in that month will see it, together with all the other devices, in operation.

The fickleness of public taste is largely responsible for the new device. A little bit of everything in the line of recreation devices, explained Mr. Solman yesterday, is the first law of a successful amusement area. And since the public always wants something different, something new must be provided. This new device, Mr. Solman said, is the first of its kind in Canada, and since the Sunnyside company controls its rights, may remain the only one, or one of just a very few, anywhere in the country.

"How much will it cost to ride?' was a natural question. In answering, Mr. Solman outlined another peculiarity of the pleasure-seeker's mind. Probably tickets will be sold at 10 cents each, or four for a quarter with the proviso that the winner gets a free ticket of entry to the next race. Most of the buyers, the genial showman prophesied, will buy the four-for-a-quarter strips, even though they may be using only one or two of them on the evening of purchase. Visitors always did that. Why, Mr. Solman did not explain, except to point out that the tickets were always good until they were used.

When Sunnyside's rides were being dismantled in late 1955, the park's original merry-go-round was shipped to the recently opened Disneyland theme park in Anaheim, California. The Derby Racer remained in Toronto and was shipped to the CNE. Although some of the special "to and from" mechanism was removed for many years, pleasure-seekers could still catch a ride on the Derby Racer during their visit to the Ex. Then, late one night some dimwits broke all the legs off the horses. The ride was immediately closed and dismantled never to race again.

Miss Toronto Contest

The management of the amusement park was always looking for something out of the ordinary to attract more and more people to what was called by many "the poor man's Riviera." Having visited Atlantic City on several occasions, the Attractions Manager put forth the suggestion that the park host a Miss Toronto contest. After all, the annual Miss America contest south of the border had been a resounding success ever since a fifteen-year-old Washington, D.C., high school student with a remarkable 30"–25"–32" figure won the first title in 1921. Even though some opposition to the idea was voiced, the proposal to hold a Miss Toronto contest was finally accepted. Then, in early 1926 advertisements were placed in the various Toronto papers outlining the requirements necessary to qualify for entry in the first Miss Toronto contest that would be held later that summer at the Sunnyside Bathing Pavilion: age – sixteen to twenty-five, marital status – single, residency – citizen of Toronto. There was an overwhelming response that first year with a total of 475 applicants seeking the title of Miss Toronto. After several preliminary contests were held in locations around town the main event followed at Sunnyside. After considerable

Finalists, 1926
Miss Toronto
Competition.

And the Winner is ...

From left to right: Helen McBride, Florence Garbe (second place), Jean Ford Tolmie (Miss Toronto, 1926), Ellis Fitzgerald, and Dorothy Asling.

deliberation the judges selected Jean Ford Tolmie, a tall, dark-eyed beauty who lived with her parents at 5 Shannon Street in the Ossington Avenue / College Street area of the city. Interestingly, Jean's name had actually been submitted by her younger brother who, fearing that his father would get upset if he saw Jean's name included in the list of contestants, used Mrs. Tolmie's maiden name and entered Jean as Jean Ford. One of the prizes awarded the new Miss Toronto was an introduction addressed to the officials of that year's Miss America contest in Atlantic City. Jean was accepted as a contestant, although she was subsequently exempted from the finals as she had not been born in the States. Nevertheless, Jean was awarded the title of Miss Congeniality.

After many years of being merely another attraction presented by the management of Sunnyside, the Miss Toronto competition was taken over in 1937 by the Toronto Police Department Amateur Athletic Association which was organized in 1883. For many years the popular event was conducted in conjunction with the Association's annual Police Games. After the amalgamation of the Toronto and area forces in 1957, the competition continued under the jurisdiction of the Metropolitan Toronto Police Amateur Athletic Association. Eventually, owing to pressure from outside sources (no contestant ever complained) the Miss Toronto competition was curtailed after Karen Johnson was selected as 1990's Miss Toronto. Over the years a total of fifty-four Miss Torontos had been selected during the Police Games. Remember the name of the first police-sponsored Miss Toronto? The year was 1937 and the winner was pretty "Billy" Hallam.

Miss Toronto Competition 1926
In the summer of 1926, a bevy of bathing beauties pose
for a panoramic camera inside the four-year-old Sunnyside Bathing Pavilion as the preliminary judging for the
first Miss Toronto title begins. The winner of the competition, Jean Ford Tolmie, is in the white bathing suit at
the extreme left of the panoramic photo.

Readied in time for the 1924 season at Sunnyside was the park's new softball diamond which was located just east of the Parkdale Canoe Club (now the Boulevard Club). Several women's leagues shared the stadium that had standing room only that first season. Rows and rows of spectators would simply assemble on the grass area outside the roped-off playing field. The games became so popular that just before the 1925 season commenced the Harbour Commission erected a number of wooden bleachers. Even this accommodation wasn't sufficient and the following year the seating was expanded by an additional 1,000 tiered seats. It wasn't unusual to have 4,000 or more fans watching teams such as the Parksides, Patricias, Grottos, Supremes, Cycles, and Parkdales play thrilling softball games at the stadium. Several thousand additional fans viewed the proceedings from atop the King Street embankment overlooking the park. Those watching from a distance saved the ten-cent price of admission. It was also in 1926 that floodlights were installed, becoming the first stadium in the city to have such modern facilities.

Sunnyside Stadium was used almost exclusively by women ball players who, as one paper wrote, were "brightly uniformed in snappy attire." The paper went on to say of one player, "As 'Buster' Nicholson of the Major League stood at the plate, brandishing her trusty war club, the opposing outfields knew they were in for a long journey."

The diversity of the various teams playing at the stadium is shown in this June 27, 1934, *Mail & Empire* article:

An extensive program covering the next five days has been planned by the Olympic Ladies' Softball League at Sunnyside. To-night Toronto Ladies and Supremes tangle in both intermediate and senior games, starting at 6:30. To-morrow, a special benefit attraction for the Fresh Air and Veterans' funds will be played, featuring a men's game between Cities Service and Sisters of Hamilton. (The Sisters were men?) Cam Ecclestone, Toronto's strike-out king, and Ed Cummings, who pitched Hamilton Wentworths and Linkeards to Ontario titles a few years back, will be the opposing pitchers. As a forerunner, Toronto Ladies meet the Maple Leafs. The bill is an attractive one and will start at 7 o'clock.

On Friday night Lakeshores meet the Maple Leafs at 6:30 while the Glen Stewarts meet the Leaf seniors at 7:45.

London Kelloggs, runners-up to Supremes for Ontario honours last year, come to town to tackle Rexalls Saturday night at 8 o'clock, while Supremes and Lakeshores meet in an exhibition game at 7. On Monday, the holiday, London plays Supremes at 3 o'clock and come right back at 8

and tackle the champions again. The evening feature will be preceded by a game between Maple Leafs and Toronto Ladies intermediates at 7 o'clock.

The largest crowd to watch the ladies play softball turned up at the park on August 17, 1938. While many were there to watch the Olympic League game, thousands turned out to see America's Sweetheart, Toronto's own Mary Pickford, who visited the stadium that evening during a short visit to her home town.

Sunnyside stadium disappeared soon after the demise of the amusement park in 1955. The site is now covered by the Boulevard Club parking lot.

Below

Tragedy struck at Sunnyside on Friday evening, June 21, 1929, when a small cotter pin on a new thrill ride called the Whoopee Wheel (a variation of the Ferris Wheel and installed at the park earlier in the year) sheared off causing several gear wheels to come loose while the ride was in operation. The jerking motion that resulted caused four riders to be thrown to the ground from two of the cars. One person, who was impaled on the picket fence that surrounded the ride, died of his injuries the following day. An inquiry was held and the occurrence was deemed an accident. When the ride was put back into operation it became known as the Swooper.

"The PLAYGROUND of TORONTO"

Merry Go Round
Flyer
Whip
Dutch Mill
Custer Cars
The Bug
Speedway
Derby Racer
Pretzel
Railway
Toboggan Wheel
Glider
Poney Track
Merrymakers
Dance Gardens
Boating
Tennis
Archery
Bowling
Lacrosse
Baseball
Lake Bathing
Pool Bathing
Golf
Kiddies' Pool

SUNNYSIDE BEACH

OFFERS

FREE RIDES

To Anyone Preserving This Preview as a Week to Week
Guide of Their Weekly Fun Menu

Two Weeks of Happiness and Hilarity

Complimentary Tickets Will be Given to Anyone Presenting This Preview in
Good Condition, Ordinary Wear and Tear Excepted, at Amusement
Office, South Side of Board Walk, Between Monday, August 15th, 1932,
and Saturday, August 27th, 1932

Glamoring Attractions Every Afternoon
and Evening

Radio
Palmistry
Weigh Scales
Bands and Orchestras
Japanese Roll Downs
Beach Chairs
Rabbit Racer
Shooting Gallery
Rose Game
Fish Pond
Bingo
Penny Games
Broadcasting
Sea Food Grill
Ball Games
High Strikers
Novelties
Dart Game
Hoop-la
Poker Games
Orthophonic
Silhouettes
Children's Playground
Kiddies' Cruiseabout
and all kinds of
REFRESHMENTS

SUNNYSIDE GARDENS
:-: RESTAURANT :-:

BOARD WALK   D. C. BURK, PROP.   TORONTO

DINNER PLATES

—Hot—

Premium Ham & Eggs with French Fried Potatoes............ 60c
"   Frankfurters   "   "   " 45c

—Cold—

Cold Roast Beef { with French Fried Potatoes............ 55c
"   Premium Ham { or Potato Salad.................... 55c
Above Orders Include Bread and Butter

SUPPER PLATES—Sundays Only

Cold Roast Beef { and French Fried Potatoes............ 25c
"   Boiled Ham { or Potato Salad.................... 25c
BURK'S FAMOUS RED HOTS............................ 10c

BEVERAGES

—Ice Cold—

White Label Ale, per pint................................ 25c
Served on Sundays with Dinner or Supper Plates only
BURK'S ORANGE DRINK. 10c   Vernor's Ginger Ale....... 10c
Hires Root Beer.......... 10c   Coca Cola............ 10c
Pot of Tea with Cream 15c.

SODA FOUNTAIN MENU

ICE CREAM SODAS 15c
Strawberry   Chocolate   Vanilla   Pineapple

PLAIN ICE CREAM 15c

PLAIN SUNDAES 20c
Strawberry   Chocolate   Vanilla   Pineapple

FRUIT AND NUT SUNDAES 25c
David Harum   Chocolate Walnut
Marshmallow Walnut
Fresh Fruit 30c

FANCY SUNDAES 35c
Sunnyside Delight   Fruited Marshmallow
Board Walk Special

SANDWICHES 15c
Ham   Salmon   Tomato & Lettuce   Cheese
Bread and Butter 10c   Assorted Cake 15c
BURK'S FAMOUS RED HOTS 10c
Pot of Tea with Cream 15c.   Individual Bottle Milk 10c

IMPORTANT
Please see that the amount of your order corresponds with the
check presented, and pay for same at the time food is served.
Report inattention to Management.
Service under ideal conditions.

Above
Centrespread from the 1932 edition of the *Sunnyside Year Book*.

Left
Known to thousands as "Cap" Burk, David Campbell Burk of 47 Davies Avenue operated several refreshment booths at Sunnyside, including the Sunnyside Gardens. Its menu is reproduced here.

Opposite
The presence of the new Sunnyside Amusement Park had quite an impact on the area's housing prices as confirmed by this realtor's advertisement that appeared in the Toronto *World* newspaper on October 8, 1922.

SUNNYSIDE!!

WORLD SUN OCT - 8 1922 8680

NO district in the City has become so popular and made such rapid strides during the past year as **SUNNYSIDE**. Thousands of people from every part of the City have taken advantage of this wonderful pleasure beach, and each year it will become more popular.

Many beautiful sites have already been secured along the water front by different Aquatic Clubs, who are erecting valuable buildings with their pretty grounds.

SUNNYSIDE development is only in its infancy. Millions of dollars will be spent in this vicinity during the next few years in Apartment Houses, Summer Hotels, etc. Could you think of a more desirable spot for your home? Near street cars, Sunnyside Station, High Park, the Lake Front Boulevard and Hamilton Highway; only 18 minutes' ride to Yonge Street, with "Roncesvalles Avenue," a good shopping district right at hand.

One year ago we offered for sale "**SUNNYSIDE HOME SITES**" immediately north of Sunnyside Beach, east from Indian Road. These have all been sold to reliable builders. We are now prepared to offer to the public some very pretty homes at popular prices.

$7300—Semi. square plan, cottage roof with fancy gables, six large rooms and spacious bathroom; beautifully finished in hardwood throughout, cut-glass hardware, high-class plumbing.

$8000—Detached, square plan, six rooms, chestnut trim, water heating, side drive.

$8300—Detached, buff brick, square plan, six rooms, well decorated, hardwood finish, two fireplaces, water heating, side drive.

$8500—Detached, cottage roof, square plan, seven rooms, hardwood finish, water heating side drive; lovely location.

$8800—Detached, bungalow style, seven rooms, beautifully constructed, all hardwood hand-rubbed and furniture finish. French doors with bevel plate-glass.

$8900—Bungalow style, seven rooms, hardwood finish throughout, tiled bathroom, water heating side drive.

$9000—Glendale Avenue, pretty home, square plan, 7 good rooms, water heating, drive; one of the best locations on the property.

$9000—Detached, bungalow front, built of Oriental brick, 7 rooms, hardwood finish throughout, tiled bath, pedestal basin, side drive. Something different.

$9500—Detached, cottage roof plan, large rooms, tiled bathroom with pedestal basin and base bath, tiled kitchen, bevelled plate glass, French doors, cut-glass hardware, water heating, large well constructed home. Good location.

$14500—Duplex residence, 6 rooms and tiled bath on each floor, all rooms are large and well lighted; exceptional location overlooking lake. Good opportunity for person wishing to occupy one apartment and rent the other. Possession about November 1st.

We have some fine store sites left on **QUEEN STREET** at very attractive prices. This property will double in value within one year.

Our temporary office **ON THE PROPERTY**, at the corner of Queen and Indian Road, will be open every afternoon during the next two weeks. Telephone for appointment.

WALLERS LIMITED

EXCLUSIVE SELLING AGENTS

JUNCTION 3007   HOUSE—JUNCTION 581 W

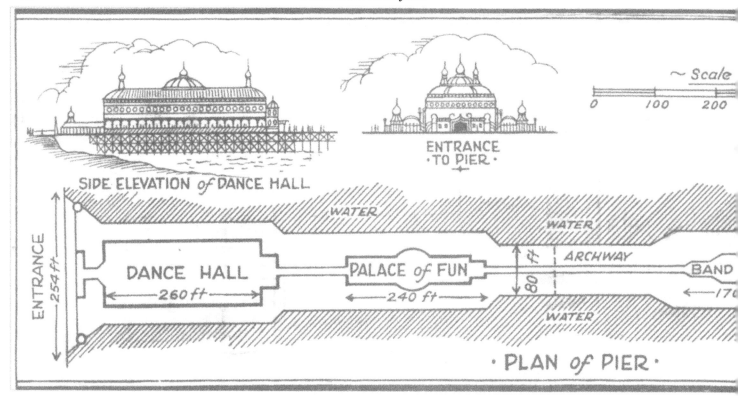

One of the most fascinating developments planned for the western beaches was what was known as the Sunnyside Palace Pier. It was a project of the Provincial Improvement Corporation whose offices were located in the Northern Ontario Building. Interestingly, this building, which still stands at the northwest corner of Bay and Adelaide streets, was designed by Alfred Chapman, the architect of the Sunnyside Bathing Pavilion.

The Palace Pier was designed by the Toronto architectural firm of Craig and Madill and was originally perceived as a $1.25 million pleasure pier, extending a half-mile out into the lake at the mouth of the Humber River. Promotional material likened the pier to the original Palace Pier in Brighton, England, and would rival in drawing power the popular Steel Pier in Atlantic City. The advertisements went on to describe the pier as being "within easy motoring distance of fifty million of the freest spenders in the world." Construction started in 1927, but financial problems, compounded by the deepening depression, forced a halt to the project in 1932 after an auditorium and only 300 feet of the pier had been completed. Nine long years of legal entanglements followed, during which time the Provincial Improvement Corporation vanished into thin air. The new Palace Pier at Humberside finally opened in 1941 as the Strathcona Roller Rink. Two years later the name was changed to The Queensway Ballroom and the roller rink became a huge dance hall. Confusion arose with the new name and the structure was soon given its original name back. Throughout the forties and fifties the big bands of Les Brown, Harry James, the Dorsey Brothers, Stan Kenton, Duke Ellington, and, of course, Toronto's own Trump Davidson filled the Palace Pier with musical favourites of the day. By 1953 tastes had changed and attractions

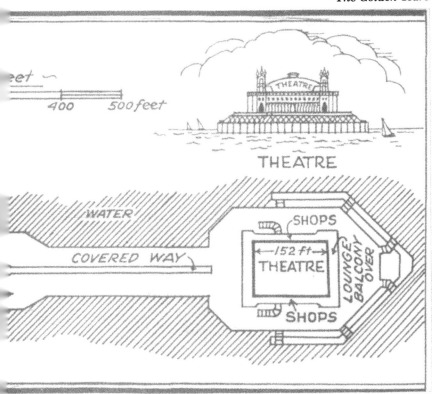

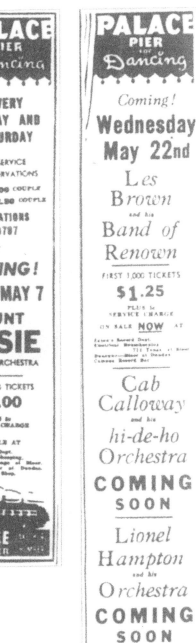

such as boxing and wrestling matches, high school proms, and religious revival meetings began to replace the big bands; except for Trump's music, that is. That went on for a few more years. Sadly, on January 7, 1963, Toronto's nostalgic Palace Pier was totally gutted by a fire that was deliberately set by a very sick individual.

High on the embankment overlooking the amusement park was a small brick railway station identified by a couple of black signs with the white letters spelling out the word "Sunnyside." Built in 1912, this station had replaced a smaller wooden station erected many years earlier by the Grand Trunk Railway. The Grand Trunk had been established in 1852 and began the first train service between Toronto and Montreal four years later. In 1882, the Grand Trunk purchased the Great Western Railway that had established a Toronto–Hamilton service in 1855. The railway erected the first Sunnyside station to serve passengers on this latter route. That station was replaced in 1912 by the brick and tile-roofed structure shown in the photograph on this and the following page. Incidentally, the Grand Trunk became part of the Canadian National Railways system in 1923.

While on the subject of roof tiles, during the period of time that the new bathing pavilion at Sunnyside was being built, the Harbour Commission's chief engineer, E.L. Cousins, paid a visit to Toronto's City Hall. There he hand-picked enough tiles from the City Hall roof (which had recently suffered severe wind damage and was being given a new copper roof) to completely cover the roof of the new bathing pavilion.

The old Sunnyside station was demolished in 1962, although the baggage doors adjacent to the mainline tracks are still evident to eagle-eyed passersby.

Former Mayor of Toronto, Art Eggleton, remembers Sunnyside with these words:

> It's interesting that as a child one remembers certain landmarks in one's hometown as immense structures. So it is that I recall the railway station at Sunnyside as almost as big as Union Station and certainly the long staircase from Roncesvalles Avenue down to the amusement park remains in my child's memory as having at least a million steps, the negotiation of each requiring the careful guidance of two parents and at least three out of four grandparents. The park itself had all the magic and excitement of a modern-day Disney World or Canada's Wonderland.

One of the best-attended attractions at Sunnyside was the Community Sing Song which was introduced in 1938 on the former Merry Makers Stage. In 1945 the event was moved to the specially designed Attractions Stage that backed onto the lake between the Sunnyside tank and Palais Royale. The following year one of the country's finest and best-known band leaders took up the baton and led the orchestra and crowds of happy singers through nine years of sing-a-longs. The late Art Hallman remembered his stint at Sunnyside with these words:

My orchestra performed at the People's Credit Jewellers Community Sing Song for ten summers, from 1946 'til 1955. Our performance took place on the Sunnyside bandshell from 8:00 pm to 9:00 pm each Sunday evening during June, July, and August. They used to call me 'the poor man's Mitch Miller.'

The last half-hour of our performance was broadcast over the Ontario Network with Toronto's CFRB the key station. People from all walks of life came out to see us and sing along. The words for the songs were printed in large letters on a huge wooden book at the back of the stage for everyone to see. We also included one hymn in our program each Sunday. Our producer was the one and only Maurice Rapkin known at that time as the 'Jingle King' as he wrote dozens of commercial jingles including the original People's Credit Jewellers' jingle. I wrote all of the music and arrangements for his commercials. Three of the girl vocalists during our time at Sunnyside were Shirley Harmer, Dorothy Deane, and Joan Fairfax. Acting as Master of Ceremonies at various times were Stan Francis, Joe Murphy, Monty Hall (of "Let's Make a Deal" fame), Michael Fitzgerald, Rick Campbell, and Don Cameron.

All the shows were extremely well attended and there was no admission fee. I personally derived much pleasure in playing and singing for the people of that time as they were starved for entertainment that the whole family could enjoy.

Known by various names, pee-wee, midget, miniature golf or in the case of Sunnyside, Tom Thumb Golf, this entertaining fad was born during the years of the Great Depression. Played on courses that came complete with Mickey Mouse or Jigs and Maggie ornaments or on a course such as the one shown here at Sunnyside, with its plaster storks and dogs and a few potted evergreens, the game was a harmless diversion from the humdrum routine of the hungry thirties. The Sunnyside Miniature Golf Course was operated as a concession by Norma and Cliff Reynolds and was located on the south side of the boardwalk, just steps east of the Palais Royale. Here we see the course on a rather quiet fall afternoon in 1939, only days before Canada was to declare war on Germany.

Sunnyside was a favourite spot for servicemen and servicewomen during the Second World War. After all, the armed forces Manning Depot No. 1 was just a short distance to the east, housed in the many buildings at the Canadian National Exhibition grounds. Here members of the RCAF occupied the Coliseum, army personnel the Horse Palace, and the navy HMCS Auto Building.

Brig. John McGinnis, the former Managing Director of the Toronto Historical Board, reminisces:

> Toronto didn't offer much in the way of entertainment for the thousands of young soldiers who flocked to Toronto during the war years, but Sunnyside was a 'meeting place' where exciting afternoons and evenings could be spent trying, usually successfully, to meet girls to share the fun the park afforded. Sunnyside was a magical place that cast its spell over the young people of my generation and provided the same appeal for us that the youth of today find at Grand Prix races or at rock concerts. And I remember well what a bitter

disappointment it was on one occasion to drive in from Camp Borden with a carload of soldier friends only to find the rides silent and the games closed for the season.

Shortly after this book appeared in the bookstores back in the fall of 1982, I received a telephone call from an agitated woman who demanded to know where I obtained the above photograph. Explaining to her my source, I asked what the problem was. Seems the airman in the front row with his arm around the young lady was her husband ... and he was supposed to be overseas!!

Another popular meeting place for military personnel was the Seabreeze. This open-air dance floor was built in 1932 on the south side of the boardwalk just a short distance east of the Sunnyside tank. It had a concrete dance floor, 210 feet by 100 feet, that was slightly sloped. Why sloped? To let rainwater run off so dancing could quickly resume once the rain let up.

In 1939, the Seabreeze came under the management of Sol Solman and Bill Cuthbert, and in 1952 the popular Jack Evans Orchestra became the "house band." The Seabreeze remained a favoured attraction right up to the end, even though "no jitterbugging or fancy dancing" was ever allowed.

SEA BREEZE

OPENS

MAY 16, 17, 18

JACK EVANS

AND HIS BAND

DANCING AT 9 P.M.

A number of boat-burning spectaculars were held in the late 1920s and early 1930s as a way of attracting visitors to the amusement park. While these promotions were popular, in hindsight they were also unfortunate with many historic Great Lakes' vessels sacrificed unnecessarily. While advertisements placed in the city's newspapers announced each coming event, those who missed the ads would probably see the searing red glow in the sky and, seeking its source, make a trip to the park. It was hoped that the visitor would spend a dollar or two while there. This type of wanton destruction is hard to understand today, as we look for remnants of our past to preserve and, if possible, to resurrect. Thank goodness the Sunnyside officials didn't get their hands on the Island ferry *Trillium*. Some of the vessels torched in the name of entertainment were the Toronto Island ferries *John Hanlan* (built 1884, burned 1929), *Jasmine* (built 1892, torpedoed, burned, and sunk 1929), *Clark Bros.* (built 1902, burned 1930), and the Great Lakes schooners *Julia B. Merrill* (built 1872, burned 1931) and *Lyman M. Davis* (built 1873, burned 1934). The *Davis* was the last of the once-numerous fleet of Great Lakes schooners. What a waste!

Sunnyside's attraction managers Don Goudy and later James Van Evera were always on the look-out for features that would entice people to visit Toronto's "playground by the lake." What follows are just a few examples of what the park offered. In 1926, just three years after the dance had been introduced in far-away Paris, Sunnyside officials held their own Charleston contest, complete with a full jazz orchestra to provide musical accompaniment. Two years later James E. Hardy, who lived not far from the park on Fuller Avenue in Parkdale, appeared at Sunnyside where he performed a thrilling high-wire act before hundreds of onlookers. As a young man, Hardy had performed several tightrope crossings of the Niagara River. In doing so he became the youngest person to ever cross the Niagara River on a high-wire. For his Sunnyside park appearance, Hardy was billed as the "Hero of Niagara Falls." Interestingly, Hardy had another Sunnyside connection. He had learned his high-wire skills by walking a wire stretched between two wooden light standards out in front of Walter Deans' first boat factory on the shore of the old Humber Bay. Chefalo, the high diver and Captain Hugo, who enjoyed driving his motorcycle through a wall of flames, appeared at Sunnyside. But they certainly weren't as popular as Alvin "Shipwreck" Kelly who wandered from city to city earning a few dollars by sitting atop a flag-pole for days on end. "Shipwreck" climbed a pole at Sunnyside on August 19, 1931. Early in his vigil a spectator informed Kelly that someone perched on a pole in New Jersey was identifying himself as *the* "Shipwreck" Kelly. The real "Shipwreck"

came down from his perch, took a train to New Jersey where he quickly tracked down the impersonator. With the enemy in his sites Kelly climbed the pole, flattened the impersonator with one punch, and returned to Toronto. Climbing back up to his perch, Sunnyside officials quickly fired him for breaking his contract. Kelly returned to the park several years later and stayed aloft for a full two weeks. Then, in 1946, the flamboyant and trusting Prince Kigor arrived at the park with his trained lions. But something must have gone amiss because just three days later the ads announced that the prince was now working with a pride of "untamed lions."

If visitors came to Sunnyside to see the spectacular attractions and to get dizzy on the Whip or Bug, they also came to the park to eat. And at Sunnyside there certainly was no lack of eating places. In 1927, the Pavilion restaurant at the west end of the amusement area offered a complete fish dinner for seventy-five cents or a full course chicken dinner for one dollar. The following year visitors could quench their thirst with Hires Root Beer or Vernor's Ginger Ale from kiosks operated by "Cap" Burk or "Sol" Solman. Sol's sons, Roy, Herbert, and Lorne, were to follow in their father's footsteps; Roy stayed with the park until the end came in 1955. Sunnyside red-hots, popcorn, peanuts, french fries in a vortex cup, and Frost Kist drinks were available at concessions all up and down the amusement strip and operated by such long-time concessionaires as Charlie Biggart, Bill Albertie, Maxie Noble, Rose Fox, and Art Keeler. One concession that many will remember was the Downyflake Donut shop near the east end of the park. It, and several others around the city, were operated by Bud Porter, nephew of long-time Sunnyside entrepreneur Lou Epstein. Epstein would open the $1.25 million Seaway Motor Hotel just west of Sunnyside in September 1954. The official ribbon-cutter on this occasion was Lorne Greene. All Downyflake shops featured a donut-making machine in the front window. Crowds would congregate in front of the restaurant window to watch as little rings of extruded white dough would plop into a vat of hot fat, sail around in a half circle until they were half done, then be flipped over by a small spatula so that the other side could be cooked. Having completed a full circle they'd be lifted out by another mechanical hand and set aside to drain and cool. At last, these delicious little beauties were ready to be washed down with a hot cup of Mother Parker's delicious coffee.

As a kid I grew up near the Bathurst/Bloor intersection where, just steps east of the old Alhambra Theatre, we had our own Downyflake shop. In fact, the first poetry I ever committed to memory was inscribed on a poster hanging in the tiny shop window. How could I ever forget the inspiring words:

As you ramble on thru life, brother,
Whatever be your goal,
Keep your eye upon the donut
And not upon the hole!

Doris Ord Fonger, who spent many evenings singing at the Club Esquire, recalls the Downyflake shop in this way:

I remember the Downyflake Donut shop that used to stand on the north side of the boulevard flanked on either side by a row of beautiful, tall poplar trees. It was the gathering place for many entertainers after their shows at the various Sunnyside stages. I was part of a girl's singing trio performing with Trump Davidson's big band. The other members were Vida Guthrie and Blanche Willis. We were performing at the near-by Club Esquire, that later became the Club Top Hat, and it was our custom to socialize at the Downyflake where the best coffee and donut in town were always available for a dime!

A BUD PORTER SHOP is an institution where nationally advertised and accepted products of quality are prepared as suggested by the manufacturers and served amid pleasant and comfortable surroundings.

Fruit and Fruit Juices

Chilled Grapefruit Juice	.10
Sun Sweet Prune Juice	.10
Iced Tomato Juice	.10

Eggs and Dairy Dishes

Two (2) strictly fresh Farm Eggs with Toast	.30
Ham, Bacon or Sausage and Two (2) Eggs, Buttered Toast	.45
Cereals of all types with Cream	.20
with Milk	.15

Fountain Specials

Sunnyside Donut Delight	.20
Ice Cream Waffle Sandwich	.10
Ice Cream Sodas (all flavors)	.20
Banana Split	.30
Butterscotch or Chocolate Sundae	.20
Large Hot Fudge Sundae	.20
Large Strawberry or Pineapple Sundae	.20
Jumbo Size Double Rich Milk Shakes, any flavor	.20
Ice Cream, per order	.15

Beverages

Blue Ribbon Coffee or Tea	.10
Blue Ribbon Coffee or Tea, Iced	.15
Hot Chocolate	.10
Milk	.10
Soft Drinks	.10

WAFFLES

Plain or Raisin

Served with Maple Syrup and Pure Creamery Butter	.25
Crushed Fruit in Season	.40
A la Mode	.35
With Ham, Bacon or Sausage or Scrambled Eggs	.40

PANCAKES

(These are really delicious!)

Served with Maple Syrup and Pure Creamery Butter	.25
With Ham, Bacon or Sausage	.40

DOWNYFLAKE DONUTS

Two (2) Plain, Cinnamon or Sugar-white Donuts with Coffee, Tea or Milk	.17
Two (2) Fancy Frosted Donuts with Coffee, Tea or Milk	.20
Donut with Ice Cream	.15

FRESH DOWNYFLAKE DONUTS TO TAKE HOME

Plain, Cinnamon and Sugar-white	doz.	.33
Fancy Frosted	doz.	.40

TAKE HOME A PACKAGE OF OUR FAMOUS WAFFLE OR PANCAKE MIX Easy to Prepare

Sandwiches (No Extra Charge for Toast)

Canadian Cheese	
Grilled Cheese	
Peanut Butter	
Fried Egg	
Tomato and Lettuce on Toast	
Bacon or Ham	
Bacon and Cheese	
Bacon and Tomato	
Western Sandwich	
Salami	
Onion Sandwich	
FRENCH FRIED POTATOES	.15
SUNNYSIDE GLORIFIED HAMBURG	.15
CHEESEBURGER	.20
GRILLED RED HOTS	.15
HOT SOUPS	.12

Downyflake Specials

Baked Beans or Spaghetti with Toast	.35
with Weiners, Bacon, Ham or Hamburg	.40
Swift's Brookfield Sausage and French Fried Pancakes with Toast or Roll	.40
Grilled Cubed Steak, French Fried Potatoes with Toast or Roll	.45
Broiled Chop Steak Platter with French Fried Potatoes, Cole Slaw and Toast	.45
Our Own Special Recipe, Corned Beef Hash with Pickle Relish, Toast or Roll	.35
Served with 1 Egg on Top	.40
French Fried Fish and Chips, Toast or Roll	.45
with above Specials, Coffee, Tea or Milk and One Donut .10	

Many thousands of visitors to Sunnyside came by streetcar. Full of eager anticipation, they would get off the cars at the always busy King / Queen / Roncesvalles / Lakeshore intersection and descended the long, steep, steel stairway to the amusement park. Actually, this stairway was built as part of the new Sunnyside traffic bridge that was erected over the railway tracks south of this busy corner in 1912, a decade before the park actually opened. The purpose of this bridge was to provide a connecting link between the intersection, that originally had just three components, Queen, King, and Roncesvalles Avenue, with the old Lake Shore Road that, in turn, joined up with the Toronto–Hamilton Highway at the Humber River.

One of the major rehabilitation projects faced by the newly established Toronto Transportation Commission was the King / Queen / Roncesvalles / Lake Shore intersection. Because hardly any maintenance work had been done on the intersection by the former transit operator, the now defunct Toronto Railway Company, the young TTC, faced a major hurdle, rebuilding what was regarded as one of the most complicated intersections on the entire continent. Crews started early in the evening of April 19, 1923, and in just nine hours all of the trackwork had been removed and replaced with new rail. Some gradient problems resulted in the City and TTC officials exchanging some harsh words. Nevertheless, the work was completed in record time and service on the *Queen*, *King*, and *Beach* routes that operated through the intersection soon resumed.

An interesting inventory of goods and services available to Torontonians of the day can be seen by examining the numerous billboards strung along the city's major thoroughfares. For example, the billboards embracing this intersection promote a veritable commercial "who's who" of the era: Cozens Spring Service, British American Gasolene and Autolene Motor Oils, Old Chum tobacco, Neilson's chocolates, the Columbia Six automobile, Laura Secord Candies, Tamblyn Drugs (same cut prices at all stores), Boulevard $1 Taxi Service, and White Brothers, Clothiers.

Opposite

Standing on the southeast corner of the King / Queen/ Roncesvalles / Lake Shore intersection was Scholes' Ocean Hotel complete with Bake-Rite Bakery, United Cigar Store, Laura Secord candy shop, and a Tamblyn drug store on the ground floor. In the lower view, taken for the original 1982 edition of this book, a ladies' wear store (a donut shop in 1996) occupied the corner, and the hotel had become an apartment building with the interesting tower lopped off. But billboards are still part of the corner and this time promote oil and tires. A now extinct PCC streetcar, westbound on the 501 route (though the eastern terminal is shown on the destination blind), clatters across the intersection. Today, streetcars in the form of Canadian Light Rail and Articulated Light Rail Vehicles continue to operate through the intersection.

Above

In the early days of Sunnyside Amusement Park, people who didn't have the good fortune to live near the park would make their way to the bathing pavilion and swimming tank via streetcars on the *Beach* route. Operating along Queen Street from the Neville Park loop in the east, the big Peter Witt streetcars, frequently hauling an equally large trailer, would, upon reaching the complex King / Queen / Roncesvalles / Lake Shore corner, veer southwesterly out over the Sunnyside bridge, descend the long incline, and continue along the Lake Shore Road. After disgorging its passengers at the bathing pavilion stop, the Witt and trailer would resume the trip to the loop over the Humber River.

In 1927 the cars were rerouted to the Sunnyside loop at Queen Street and Sunnyside Avenue, and on June 11 of the following year to the new Parkside loop, just west of the Pavilion Restaurant (later the site of the Club Esquire, then the Club Top Hat). Later in the year another new route, *Lakeshore*, was inaugurated providing service from downtown Toronto via Lake Shore Road and the park, to Long Branch in Etobicoke Township. On August 2, 1937, this route became part of the new *Queen* service which on July 21, 1957, was taken off Lake Shore Road (and away from what was left of the park) and began operating over track laid on a private right of way in the centre of the newly built Queensway.

Traditionally, the Sunnyside Amusement Park season
began on Victoria Day and ran until Labour Day. But one
could always find the odd refreshment stand or ride operating in late April or early May and still be going strong
well into October. Winter, however, was another thing.
Here in the winter of 1932, the merry-go-round and a
windmill-less Dutch Mill sit under a covering of snow quietly awaiting the first eager throngs of merrymakers who
would almost certainly arrive at the park just about the
same time the snow and ice began to melt.

During the warmer months this intersection was filled with young couples heading for the Sunnyside rides, youngsters with bathing suits and towels rushing to the bathing tank, and grandmothers and grandfathers intent on reaching Merton Plunkett's Merrymakers Stage in time for the first act. Here, having just ascended the Sunnyside bridge, a large Witt streetcar on the *Beach* route stops to pick up a couple of bone-chilled passengers in the dead of winter, 1927.

To the left is the Sunnyside railway station and restaurant and in the distance, beside the lone pedestrian, the entrance to the long steep stairway down to the park. To the right of centre is the public lavatory and local taxi-cab office that were also landmarks at this intersection for many years.

The death knell for the amusement park was sounded in 1948, but everyone was having so much fun they didn't hear it. In that year a subcommittee of the City of Toronto's Planning Department recommended a $12 million super-highway be built along the waterfront from the Humber River to Woodbine Avenue, a modern thoroughfare that would cut right through the heart of the city's "playground by the lake." But the music kept playing, the carousel kept whirling, and the swimmers kept swimming. "What's this about some sort of new highway?"

The four photographs on these two pages show the amusement park in its post–Second World War days. **(Above)** Directing Lakeshore Boulevard traffic is one of the city's finest who has recently been issued the new "forage-style" head gear that was slowly, but surely, replacing the traditional "bobby" helmet. Officers wearing this latter head gear could no longer fit comfortably in the modern, more streamlined police cars. **(Below)** Crowds at the west end of the park stroll past Rose Fox's refreshment stand, and the Auto Ride and the Aeroplane Swingaround.

Above
Mom and the kids, spending a leisurely day at Sunnyside, wander past the games arcade ("Come back junior!") towards one of the park's first rides, the always popular merry-go-round, while **(below)** that salesman from up the street sits and watches the ever-increasing traffic on the Lakeshore Boulevard whiz by. Planners realized that this worsening traffic situation had to be addressed and they recommended the construction of a super-highway. With the park's future very much an uncertainty the park landlord, the Toronto Harbour Commission, put the concessionaires on year-to-year leases. It was obvious; the end was in sight.

Late one cold November evening in 1955 flames were discovered licking at the footings of the old wooden roller-coaster. The fire department responded and the flames quickly dowsed. But this was the third suspicious fire in less than a month and this time lives were nearly lost. Officials of the Toronto Harbour Commission reacted quickly and within weeks Sunnyside was no more.

Five
The Death of Sunnyside

In the years that followed the end of the Second World War, traffic volumes on the streets leading into and out of the city increased to staggering numbers. Before long it wasn't unusual to see the traffic on Lakeshore Boulevard in the vicinity of Sunnyside at a complete standstill. It was obvious something had to be done.

For years rumours had been making the rounds that the city was considering the construction of a new limited access multi-lane highway that would connect The Queen Elizabeth Highway with downtown Toronto. These rumours were more than just someone speculating, for when the new Municipality of Metropolitan Toronto was created in 1953 it was given the responsibility of building major highways in and around Metro, and the so-called Lakeshore Expressway was high on its list. Engineering drawings began to give the concept a definite appearance and, yes, it would be built right through the heart of the amusement park. But that possibility, now fact, didn't really stir much in the way of controversy. Perhaps Toronto had become too important and now Sunnyside was just in the way. Besides, the crowds had certainly dropped off now that gasoline and tires were no longer rationed and the desire to get out on the roads and see other people and places became more prevalent. The uncertainty over Sunnyside's future caused the park's physical appearance to deteriorate rapidly. Paint peeled, weeds grew, and the battered old wooden boardwalk soon became virtually impassable. To compound the problems faced by the concessionaires, the park's landlord began extending their leases for only a single year. And something else happened, only this time the event went almost unnoticed. The park's lovely old merry-go-round was quietly sold to someone named Walt Disney who was building the world's first theme park down in Anaheim, California. In 1954, a portion of the boardwalk was replaced by an asphalt strip and plans were bandied about to move the park's rides and games to Toronto Island or High Park or the Ex or anywhere. One evening in early November 1955, following a semi-successful season at the park, a small fire broke out in one of the concession buildings near the roller-coaster. It was quickly brought under control. Several days later a larger fire was detected and again the fire department responded. Could these fires have been deliberately set? A few weeks went by without incident and then on November 24 a major blaze quickly consumed several buildings under the Flyer. When it was discovered that several youngsters had been trapped inside one of the buildings it was obvious that this fire could have been much more serious. Dozens of rescue vehicles responded and while the firefighters' efforts were successful, the resulting traffic jam was one of the worst the city had ever seen. That near disaster sealed the park's fate. "Sunnyside is a definite safety hazard," commented William Bosley, Chairman of the Toronto Harbour Commission. "Something must be done, and quickly." That "something" was an immediate call for tenders for the demolition of all the buildings at Sunnyside. The request was issued on November 26, the demolition contract awarded on December 5, and by late February 1956 the site had been cleared. Sunnyside, as most people knew it, was dead.

Today, more than forty years after Sunnyside's last full season, only the Palais Royale dance hall, the swimming tank, and the bathing pavilion are left as memorials of a time when Torontonians found time to dance under the stars, go for a stroll along the boardwalk, munch candy floss and red-hots, ride the merry-go-round and roller-coaster ... the list is endless. Unfortunately, Sunnyside was not.

"One of the Pavilion's outside gardens is truly Italian, resembling a Venetian garden divided off in terraces and sections. Admission is only 75¢ and includes refreshments and dancing under the stars." So wrote a local newspaper reporter in the summer of 1921 when Sunnyside's Pavilion Restaurant was one of the city's "in" places. Eventually, the building would enjoy a new career: first as the Club Esquire, then as the Club Top Hat. The building was to fall on rough times, however, and was eventually pulled down to make way for a new waterfront superhighway.

"Just what makes two hearts beat in three-quarter time to the rhythm of klunking feet on boards, civic officials have no idea, but they are ready to resist efforts to replace the boardwalk with any substitute." Thus wrote the City Hall reporter for the Toronto *Telegram* newspaper. Spearheading efforts to retain the boardwalk at Sunnyside was a city official with an extraordinarily appropriate name, Parks Commissioner Walter Love. But, as the park began to lose its popularity, even the once-sacred wooden planks of the boardwalk, all 11,964 of them, became mere sentinels of a fading past.

In this photograph, taken in the fall of 1954, a Consumers' Gas workman pays scant attention to tradition as he manipulates his saw through the worn planks of the Sunnyside boardwalk in preparation for the installation of a new natural gas pipeline along Lakeshore Boulevard. Recently, the city has rebuilt portions of the Sunnyside boardwalk with TREX, a material that looks and feels somewhat like wood, but is actually a new product formulated out of recycled plastics.

Opposite

The end is very near and two of Sunnyside's many concession buildings look even more tired than they had the previous winter.

Following the third fire in less than three weeks (the last blaze requiring a second alarm to be rung in), William H. Bosley, Chairman of the Toronto Harbour Commission, stated, "It is clearly the duty of the Commission to remove all of those buildings and the wooden roller-coaster as quickly as possible. We will start now." This newspaper notice was placed in the City's dailies on November 26, 1955. It read, in part:

Tenders for Wrecking Buildings

Tenders for demolition of buildings, structures and erections in the amusement area of Sunnyside Beach will be received until 10 A.M. on November 29th, 1955.

Only a few tenders were received in response to the notice and only a Brantford, Ontario, firm offered the Commission any remuneration for scrap materials. As a result, on December 5, 1955, a demolition contract was awarded to Kepic Brothers who paid the Commission a total of $335 for all that was left of Toronto's "playground by the lake," tired old Sunnyside.

TENDERS
FOR WRECKING BUILDINGS

For demolition and removal of buildings, structures and erections in the Amusement Area of Sunnyside Beach, Toronto.

Sealed tenders, addressed to the Toronto Harbour Commissioners, 60 Harbour Street, Toronto 1, and marked "Tender for Demolition of Buildings," will be received until 10 o'clock in the morning, Tuesday, 29th November, 1955, for the demolition and removal of buildings, etc., at Sunnyside Beach.

Plans and Specifications can be seen at Office No. 114 of the Toronto Harbour Commissioners, 60 Harbour Street, Toronto.

Tenders will not be considered unless made on the forms supplied by the Toronto Harbour Commissioners and in accordance with the conditions as set forth therein.

Each tender must be accompanied by a certified cheque on a chartered bank in Canada, payable to the Toronto Harbour Commissioners, equal to the tender price.

Any or all tenders not necessarily accepted.

The Commissioners will supply plans and specifications of the work on deposit of a sum of Twenty-Five ($25.00) Dollars in the form of a certified bank cheque, payable to the order of the Toronto Harbour Commissioners.

The deposit will be released on the return of the plans and specifications within a month from the date of the reception of tenders. If plans and specifications are not returned within that period, the deposit will be forfeited.

E. B. GRIFFITH,
General Manager.

Goin' ...

Goin' ...

Gone ...

Opposite

Once the offer submitted by the Kepic Brothers of Brantford, Ontario, had been accepted by the Harbour Commission, the company wasted no time in getting to work and within weeks Sunnyside was no more. As the work of clearing the site progressed the following editorial appeared in the January 23, 1956 edition of the Toronto *Star*:

All the arguments over whether [the rides at] Sunnyside should be moved having ended with a decision that [they] should, workmen are now busy tearing down the old buildings. It is a good thing, of course, to get the rickety roller-coaster, the merry-go-round, the miniature auto course and the assorted hot dog and lemonade stands out of the way. They were in the path of the new Lake Shore expressway. Nothing can be permitted to hold up progress.

But, somehow, we can't help feeling a little sorry to see the old place go. For more than 30 years Sunnyside has been a familiar Toronto landmark, a favourite meeting place, a happy playground for children and a naively glamorous 'hangout' for teen-agers. It will be missed.

Back in the 1920s, when cars had running boards and women bobbed their hair and boldly displayed their knees Sunnyside was a wonderful place to flirt with flappers and feast on nickel hot dogs. During the depression it became the unemployed man's Riviera. A part of the city's 1934 relief work program was the construction of a new boardwalk at a cost of $26,400. This gave employment to a foreman, eight carpenters, and ten labourers.

There has been talk of moving Sunnyside to the CNE grounds or the Island. But the future is uncertain. Actually, when the wreckers get finished there won't be anything to move. The Harbour Commission, which owns both the land and the concessions, apparently is not interested in continuing in the carnival business. Youngsters will be glad to hear that the Kiddieland attractions south of the Lakeshore Blvd. will remain where they are.

Private interests may set up another summer playground. But the Sunnyside of our youth has all but vanished. The long, cool evenings, the noise and colour, the good times will live in the memories of a generation.

Above

The playground where once happy throngs gathered was, by early 1956, a barren wasteland. Soon highway construction crews would demolish the remaining Sunnyside Bridge and connect up the old Lake Shore Road running through the west end of the amusement park with Lakeshore Boulevard at a point opposite the Palais Royale. Several years later the Lakeshore Expressway, not surprisingly renamed the Gardiner Expressway by the time the first workmen appeared on the scene, would be laid out through the area to the left of this photograph.

After thirty-three happy seasons (admittedly, some happier than others) the Sunnyside amusement park that thousands of Torontonians had known and loved was no more. In its place were acres of dusty fields and the occasional mud hole. And as work progressed nearby on Toronto's new waterfront expressway, showman extraordinaire Paddy Conklin and his son Jim tried to keep some sort of life in the area by operating something called Kiddieland on the south side of Lakeshore Boulevard. But politicians, construction crews, and their huge vehicles combined with the dangerously over-crowded traffic boulevard that cut the small amusement area off from the city all acted against the success of the Conklin venture.

Renovated, rejuvenated, and renamed King Arthur's Carousel, the old Sunnyside merry-go-round continues to entertain new generations of pleasure-seekers at Disneyland in Anaheim, California.

Immediately following the removal of all the Sunnyside rides and buildings, work began on the dismantling of the old Sunnyside bridge. At the top right of this 1956 aerial view is a portion of what is now known as St. Joseph's Health Centre. John Howard's Sunnyside villa originally stood in amongst the trees that appear in this photo between the hospital and the new Queensway. The hospital's large parking garage now stands on this site.

To the right of centre is the Toronto Transit Commission's Roncesvalles carhouse with dozens of PCC and Peter Witt streetcars filling the yard. The carhouse opened in 1923 replacing an older, obsolete facility erected by the Commission's predecessor, the Toronto Railway Company, in 1895.

At the centre bottom is the Sunnyside CNR station and the overhead pedestrian bridge that conveyed travellers to and from the eastbound and westbound tracks. Adjacent is the King / Queen / Roncesvalles intersection now minus its Lake Shore link but augmented by the new Queensway connection.

The concept of a new cross-waterfront expressway was first mentioned as early as 1948. At that time the price tag was pegged at $12 million. But it wasn't until March 1955 that the elected officials of the newly created Municipality of Metropolitan Toronto Council gave final approval to the construction of what would become a $103,500,000 mega-project. By the spring of 1957 the right of way from the Humber River to the Exhibition grounds had been cleared and several bridge structures built.

The first stretch of the Gardiner Expressway, from the Humber River to Spencer Avenue, opened on August 8, 1959. The elevated section from Spencer Avenue to the Don Valley Parkway opened November 6, 1964 and the stretch from the Parkway to Leslie Street on July 6, 1966. There was to be a connecting link from Leslie Street northeast to Highway 401. This so-called Scarborough Expressway has yet to materialize.

This 1957 photo shows extensive clearing and grading operations prior to the construction of the new west-bound lanes of the Lakeshore Boulevard through Sunnyside. To the left of centre the Sunnyside bridge is being dismantled and in the centre background the Pavilion Restaurant/Club Esquire/Club Top Hat has vanished.

Sunnyside Beach, September 1996.
In this aerial view taken during the busy morning rush hour by CHFI's traffic reporter, Darryl Dahmer, we see the site of the once-popular Sunnyside Amusement Park a little more than four decades after it was overtaken by the new and fast-growing Metropolitan Toronto. Visible in the photograph are (clockwise from top left) Grenadier Pond, High Park, St. Joseph's Health Centre, the TTC's Roncesvalles carhouse, the King / Queen / Roncesvalles / Queensway intersection, a few of the residences of south Parkdale (then, crossing King Street, the rail corridor, the six lanes of the Gardiner Expressway, and six lanes of the Lakeshore Boulevard), the Boulevard Club, the Palais Royale (at the south end of the $250,000 pedestrian bridge erected in 1958), and, where it all began seventy-four years ago, the bathing pavilion and nearby swimming tank.

After years of neglect the City of Toronto, spurred on by the Parkdale Village Foundation, a local citizens' group, appropriated just over $1 million to partially restore the Sunnyside Bathing Pavilion, built in 1922. On June 14, 1980, following extensive renovations to the roof and locker facilities and refurbishing of the exterior walls, the Bathing Pavilion was officially rededicated. In the summer of 1996 the Sunnyside Cafe opened in the historic building.

Six
As Others Pictured Sunnyside

When this book went out of print several years ago, I began seeking out a publisher who might be willing to undertake the production of a revised edition. When Dundurn Press' Kirk Howard agreed to include the book in the company's Fall 1996 catalogue, I suggested we add a selection of "people pictures" that had been taken by plain, ordinary visitors to Sunnyside. To seek out some of these candid shots I asked readers of my Toronto *Sunday Sun* "The Way We Were" column (that has been a popular feature of "the little paper that grew" since 1975) to take a look through their old photo scrapbooks and see if any pictures of the park might still exist. Surprisingly, even though more than forty years have gone by since the park closed and the last of those Sunnyside photos was pasted down in the family scrapbook, several readers came up with photos they had snapped with the family Kodak Brownie, or Hawkeye camera one warm summer's day a lifetime ago at good old Sunnyside Amusement Park. Unfortunately, as happens with many photos of this type, they get put away without identifying either those in the photo or the date that the picture was taken. Still, the following selection of candid photos gives us a feeling for Sunnyside that's often missing in professional photographs. Enjoy.

From Clarence Dungey.

From Jerry Druchok (top row, fifth from left).

Anonymous donation.

All three from Ken Maxwell.

From Clarence Dungey.

From Clarence Dungey.

From Gladys Hursh.

Anonymous donation.

Anonymous donation.

From Clarence Dungey.

Bibliography

Filey, Michael. *Trillium and Toronto Island*. Toronto: Peter Martin Assoc., 1976.

Guillet, E.C. *Toronto: From Trading Post to Great City*. Toronto: Ontario Publishing Company, 1934.

Kidd, G.; Erb. N.; Filey, M. *Once Upon a Century*. Toronto: J.H. Robinson Publishing Limited, 1978.

Kyriazi, G. *The Great American Amusement Parks*. Secaucus, N.J.: Citadel Press, 1976.

Martyn, Lucy. *Toronto, Toronto*. Toronto: Gage, 1980.

McNamara, H.; Lomas, J. *The Bands Canadians Danced To*. Toronto: Griffin House, 1973.

Miles. *Illustrated Historical Atlas*. County of York, 1878.

Parkdale Centennial Research Committee. *Parkdale*. Toronto: Published by the Committee, 1978.

Plewman, W.R. *Adam Beck and The Ontario Hydro*. Toronto: Ryerson, 1947.

Pursley, Louis. *Toronto Trolley Car Story*. Los Angeles: Interurbans, 1961.

———. *Street Railways of Toronto*. Los Angeles: Interurbans, 1958.

Scadding, Henry. *Toronto of Old*. Toronto: Stevenson & Co., 1873.

Sister Agnes. *The Congregation of the Sisters of St. Joseph*. Toronto: St. Joseph's Convent, 1951.

West, Bruce. *Toronto*. Toronto: Doubleday, 1979.

Photo Credits:
All photographs are from the author's collection and are used with thanks to the Toronto Harbour Commission Public Affairs Department (for photos on pages 2, 48, 50, 51 both, 54, 55, 56, 57, 59 all, 61, 63, 64 both, 66 both, 67 top, 68, 69, 70, 72, 74, 75 both, 76, 77, 78, 79, 80, 81 both, 82, 86, 94 both, 95, 98, 108, 110, 111, 112 bottom, 113, 114, 115, 119, 120, 122, 123, 126, 128, 130, 131, 132 both, 134, 135, 136), the Toronto Transit Commission Archives (21, 22, 23 both, 24, 31, 42, 43, 71, 90, 92, 93, 112 top, 116, 117), the City of Toronto Archives (10, 39, 41, 45, 46 bottom, 47 bottom, 84, 96, 97), Toronto *Sun*, Toronto *Telegram* collection (73, 85, 86 bottom, 87, 99, 102 bottom, 124, 127, 137), Metro Toronto Reference Library, (34, 37), Canadian National Exhibition Archives (15), St. Joseph's Health Centre Archives (32).

Thanks to:
Christine Ardern
Harry Boyle
David Crombie
Darryl Dahmer
Jerry Druchok
Clarence Dungey
Doris Ord Fonger
David Garrick
Elwood Glover
Dennis Haigh
Art Hallman
Gladys Hursh
Sister Janet
Bill Jones
Ben Kayfetz
Irene Lux
Ruth Mathews
Ken Maxwell
Ed Mirvish
Anthony Ormsby
Lois Paulson
Linda Price
Steve Roberts
Sam Sniderman
Ted Wickson
and the nice people at Henry and Company and Charles Abel Photo Finishing.
And special thanks to Kirk Howard, Nadine Stoikoff, and Ron Rochon of Dundurn Press, and to my wife Yarmila who typed both the original and revised manuscripts, proofed all the text, and was always there to listen and advise.